Flying High

A PARSI LIFE OF GRATITUDE

37 amazing true stories stranger than fiction

by

Noshir N Sanjana

INDIA · SINGAPORE · MALAYSIA

ISBN
Paperback 979-8-89632-474-4
Hardcase 979-8-89673-341-6

Without the unfailing support, the boundless love, and the unflagging encouragement of my dearest wife and soulmate Maloo, my dearest, darling daughters, Zeena & Jennifer, their wonderful life partners Mehernosh & Serge, my beautiful grandchildren Kaizia, Kayan and Gisele, this book would never have been written, nor ever published.

Thanks to my most beloved late parents, Jala & Nader; my mentor, my guiding light, my brother Rusi; and my best friend and well-wisher, my sister Lily, my life was and is one long story of love, joy, happiness, and adventure.

I would like to thank my publishers, Becomeshakespeare. com, their most actively involved project manager, Ms Miral Bheda, the "go-to-person" when in trouble Ms Trupti Sawardekar and my very warm and caring editor, Ms Sita Bhaskar, who burnt the midnight oil, and put her heart and soul to make my book come alive.

Love what you do,
and you will not work a single day in your life.

Confucius

Caption:

My parents were at a dance party in a fancy dress competition. Hence my dad is dressed as a Maharajah.

I dedicate this book to my dearest & most loving parents,

Jala Nader Sanjana

&

Nader Jehangir Sanjana

My dearest mother and

my dearest father

when I think of you both,

I am reminded of an old song:

Mother & Father of mine,

you gave to me,

all of my life, to do as I pleased

I owe everything I have, to you

sweet mother, sweet father of

of mine.

-Noshir N. Sanjana

About the Author

Noshir Sanjana has several loves in his life: love for family, love for Air India (version 1.0), love for the city of Bombay (Mumbai). But the love of writing came late in life; during the pandemic when the world was forced into social isolation and Noshir was able to look at a life well lived in the rear-view mirror. His constant companion, Samsung Galaxy A 71 Mobile, became the recipient of his stories, which metamorphosed into his first novel in stories – Flying High.

Noshir lives in Mumbai, India, but his heart travels to New York and Toronto, to share his love for family with his siblings.

Contents

1

The Burning Blue Cupboard

We lived on the top floor of the Grand Hotel, a four-star hotel in Shimla. As grand as its name, it was a magnificent brown-and-gold wood and stone building that stood on a snow-capped mountain.

My father was a junior partner and also the General Manager of the hotel. His senior investment partner was a Sikh gentleman. He was the main investor and the sleeping partner.

From the first stone laid to the last wooden beam posited the construction of the hotel was my father's dream project. After it was built, he knew every staff member that he recruited; from the maali (gardener) all the way up to the Senior Commercial Manager. He trained everyone: the Accounts Manager, the Head Chef, the Chief Security Officer, and was responsible for the smooth functioning of the hotel.

We lived in perfect harmony from the early 1940s through the Second World War, and into 1947, up to the days leading to the partition. But before our very eyes, Shimla, slowly but surely, turned into an ongoing battlefield.

I was five years old and spent my days in idyllic childhood play. My sister Lily was eight, and my brother Rusi was fourteen.

My world was enveloped in my huge blue toy cupboard. In it, I could get lost in board games like Snakes & Ladders, and Ludo. I also had a carrom-board, a chess set, a jar of multi-coloured and shiny glass marbles, a plastic cricket bat, a tennis ball, and a tiny pair of boxing gloves. I knew nothing of what was happening to my half-asleep, half-awake town. This beautiful, very icy and wintery, frosty, and snowy, Shimla. This town that looked like a huge, white canvas oil painting.

Being on the border of what was to be partitioned as 'India and Pakistan', Shimla became a war disaster zone. The inherent religious and cultural differences between the Hindus and the Muslims broke out into a hostile, maddening, unholy, Godless all-out war. With the imminent Hindu-Muslim dislodgement and the expulsions of the population due to the partition looming ahead, a trail of blazing fires lit up the skies. Shimla was burning, like Rome in the days of Emperor Nero.

The rioters, looters, marauders, and plunderers left behind a trail of burning buildings, burned down hotels, over-turned cars, flaming buses, scorched carcasses, and corpses, turning into charcoal, in humongous flames and wildfires.

Brutality and cruelty were on a rampage and crimson-red blood flowed in my Shimla. The mob had turned slayers and butchers, arsonists and pyromaniacs. Men armed with swords, knives, and flaming torches were running amok. There was rage and fury, everywhere. Bodies were hacked, tossed, strewn, and scattered everywhere. There was slaughter, annihilation, and massacre, wherever you looked.

Muslims killing Hindus!

Hindus killing Muslims!!

Men killed men.

Men killed women.

Men killed children.

In sheer madness and frenzy.

The most common outbursts and outcry heard were:

"Kitney Hindu maaray, saalay?" (How many bloody Hindus did you kill?)

"Saaray Musalman ko kaat dalo" (Chop and kill all the Muslims!!)

No five-year-old should witness the carnage I saw.

Heads chopped off.

Bodies cut in half.

Our lovely home in Grand Hotel perished when the hotel was completely burned down to the ground. The flames devoured all our family belongings: my mom's jewellery, cash, bank accounts, various ownership documents, and all our valuables.

We fled.

My father strapped his 12-bore rifle, made in England, over his shoulder, and carried me and my sister in his arms. My mother, in a night gown, grasped my brother's hand and tried to keep up with my father. Where were we going? I did not know. To my five-year-old mind, the burning of my blue toy cupboard was more devastating than the headless bodies and the screaming mob.

We were accosted, halted, and challenged by the mob with flaming torches and other weapons in hand, to find out if we were Hindus or Muslims.

"Parsis," my father shouted above the din, as if we were aliens from another planet.

They had never heard of Parsis. "Hindu-Parsi or Muslim-Parsi?" they shouted, in their ignorance.

My dad changed his answer after quickly identifying the religion of his accosters, won them over using every trickery and ploy he knew, to convince and satisfy the opposing gangs.

We took refuge for a few days with the family of a very close Sikh friend of my father, living in the basement shelter hideaway. Our two families subsisted on a bag of rice, atta (flour) for chapatis, ghee, and goat milk from their pet goats.

When all the elders thought it was safe, we made our way to the railway station and were soon on a train to Bombay. Like us, refugees from the violence were packed into every nook & corner of the train, including hanging outside, on the roof of the compartments. I had never seen such crowds in Shimla. Where did they all come from? Had they all lived in Shimla?

We were not completely safe because, the killing and dousing victims with gasoline and setting them on fire continued on the train, until we were far, far away, and closer to Bombay. My mother and father tried to shield us from these horrific acts, but we were too young and our curiosity got the better of us.

A few panic-filled days and nights later, our bedraggled family of five castaways and hobos, looking down-and-out, homeless and vagrant, reached Bombay Central Station.

I do not know how my father had managed to contact them, but my mother's two favourite brothers, Vicoo and Nusli maama, and my dad's brother, Naval kaka, were at the station to welcome us.

My mom broke down into loud sobs in the arms of her brothers, and they held her in a tight embrace as if they would never let her go. My mom's pent-up anxiety, suppressed, stored, and stockpiled with fear and pain over the weeks, was released on the railway platform.

Later, she said they were tears of joy and newfound happiness.

Witnessing a few hundred brutal killings, mass destruction, loss of property and valuables, vicious violence and catastrophic disaster did not break my mom and dad's spirit.

To survive this hell, this living nightmare and horror, my dad needed a heart of steel, a mind, with the sharpness of a Samurai sword, and muscles of bronze.

All of which, he showed us in his actions to save us.

My mom needed to match that. She had held on for the past few weeks to remain in tune with my father, to show him and us, that she too was made of strong metal.

For all of us, it was like being born again.

The biggest horror movie of my young life had come to an end with a very happy ending.

On my part, I missed my whole world in the big, blue cupboard.

On some nights, I had nightmares of a burning blue cupboard, and my toys helping each other to escape from the orange flames of destruction.

2

Back to Bombay at Grandma Motamai's Cottage

We arrived in Bombay, homeless and penniless. With middle-age looming on the horizon, my parents found that they had lost everything they had, everything they owned. All gone in a jiffy in the blazing inferno that was once the snow-white town of Shimla.

At the age of 38 my father had to build a life from scratch for himself, his wife, and his three children. In the midst of all the turmoil in the country, he had to get a new job or set up a new business to start his life all over again. But he had no time to brood and worry about the future. His biggest asset was the love and the warm welcome extended with open arms by both his and my mother's side of the family. They were settled in Vakola, Santacruz East, and also Dadar.

We were urged to settle down in my grandmother's six-bedroom joint family home in Vakola, Santacruz East. The other side of the family, not to be outdone, our eldest uncle and aunt, Vicajee mama and Goola maami invited us to live with them in Parsi Colony, Dadar. So many choices when people in other parts of the country were still trying to decipher the meaning of home and where they belonged.

After much discussion, my parents decided to stay in the beautiful countryside home, Motamai Cottage in Vakola.

The cottage was surrounded by more than two acres of green land - green grass and canopies of greener trees. I was fascinated by the coconut trees - tall and arched, my eyes they looked like sinewy serpents reaching to the sky. There were drumstick trees with twelve to twenty-four inches of hanging green drumsticks. We also had many imli (tamarind), sitaphal (custard apple) and chikoo (sapodilla) trees.

But, the prized possession was a giant Alfonso mango tree. The mangoes were not allowed to ripen. My aunts plucked the mangoes before their time to make mango pickles. If a few extra ones were left, we would eat them katcha (raw). They were also very khatta (sour) which caused our teeth to tingle and one eye to close when we bit down on them. For years later, I always thought that it was a requirement to shut one eye while eating raw green mangoes.

Among the trees were big, very sharp, and thorny bushes of sweet and sour khatta 'bore' (purple berries). I never thought of the thorns when I crawled through those bushes to pluck berries, but I would spend painstaking hours pulling out the many razor-sharp thorns that would pinch, poke, and get lodged in my arms and legs.

"When you plunge into the bushes for berries, do you forget there are thorns?" my mother asked, when I went to her whining about thorns and showing her the scratches. She soothed my scratches with calamine lotion.

"They should make bushes without thorns," I complained.

My mother walked me to the farm animals to distract my mind from the painful scratches.

Our little farm was a home to a few billy goats with beards, some female goats, a flock of native chickens, and some very beautiful and graceful roosters. We depended on the goats for their milk and the chickens for their protein- rich brown -shelled eggs.

We had a deep, clear water well, with steps made from rocks going around the inner wall. My brother Rusi, my favourite cousins Sohrab and Maneck, and one daring uncle Noshir mama, often dived in and paddled around in the crystal-clear water in the summer heat. "Where does the water come from?" I asked. They told me that the bottom of our well was interlinked with underwater streams and tributaries, connecting to the Mithi river close by.

Motamai Cottage in Vakola was a paradise in every way except one. The toilets. There were no indoor toilets. We had to use one of the two outdoor toilets. At my age, it was scary and very worrisome each time I had to answer nature's call. The toilets were at the end of a long grassy path that had been made walkable by placing broken and uneven tiles. This path was quite tricky to negotiate in the dark. During the rains, the path became slushy and slippery. It seemed like we were walking to the end of the world.

The outdoor tin-roofed toilet cabins were built on a raised platform. There were no flush tanks and no automatic flush mechanisms, and definitely no gleaming white ceramic commodes of today. We had to squat on a flat platform over a large oval hole between our two feet. This was known as "the Indian style." The toilets had very large heavy duty plastic barrels placed underneath to collect the daily human waste.

My uncle, Dhunjishaw mama, employed workers known as mehters, or binmen, to clear the daily garbage and dry refuse. They would come every day around noon from behind the toilet cabins to take away the day's refuse and leave an empty barrel in place.

In my anxiety to spend as little time as possible Indian style, I raced through my business and ran out of the cabin every day.

But one unfortunate morning, the same haste caused my foot to slip on the platform, and before I knew it, I was in deep doo-doo – five years old and up to my chest in the offerings of my larger-than-life family. Luckily, in spite of all the stench threatening to suffocate me, I was able to open my mouth and scream.

If my elder sister, Lily, was not my darling till then, that day she became my darlingest elder sister. She was next in line, waiting outside the toilet cabin. She rushed inside and used all her eight-year-old strength to pull me out. Lily to the rescue! Both of us were a blubbering mess – me, bawling that if she did not get me out, I would have to wait till the mehters came at noon to remove the barrel, and Lily terrified that she, too, would be sucked into the barrel while trying to pop me out.

Somehow she managed to walk me back to the cottage mori (bathing room). She sprayed and washed me with a long hose pipe as if I was a car that had rolled into a swampy ditch. The water was cold, and I howled and shivered. She bathed me with buckets and buckets and buckets of warm water. With each bucket, she soaped me down with a bright red bar of Lifebuoy soap. By the time she was done, the soap had become a small sliver. She told me to wait in the bathroom and ran into the main house. She returned with my mother's talcum powder box – something that was sparingly used and dusted on lightly only for special occasions. I was not happy until Lily had emptied close to half the box on my little-but-not-so-stinking body, after which I stepped back into the house and entered the living room, exuding the pleasant fragrance of my mother's talcum powder – a far cry from smelling of the collective excrement of the entire family.

My Indian style disappearance became a joke in the family. For days, wherever I went, everyone pinched their nose and ran out of the room. None of my uncles and aunts would let me come within ten feet of them! I got no hugs, no lap time, no fondling, no kisses from anyone except my darlingest Lily. She alone knew the transformation she had achieved. To the others, it was a joke; to a five-year-old, it was sad and hurtful.

I never ventured alone to the toilet cabin for a very long time. I would only go if my sister Lily accompanied me.

Till today, I do not know if Lily pulled me back up through the hole or raced behind the cabin and pulled me out from the barrel. In my terror, I blanked out what happened, and it remains one of the mysteries of my life.

3

A Gullible Boy

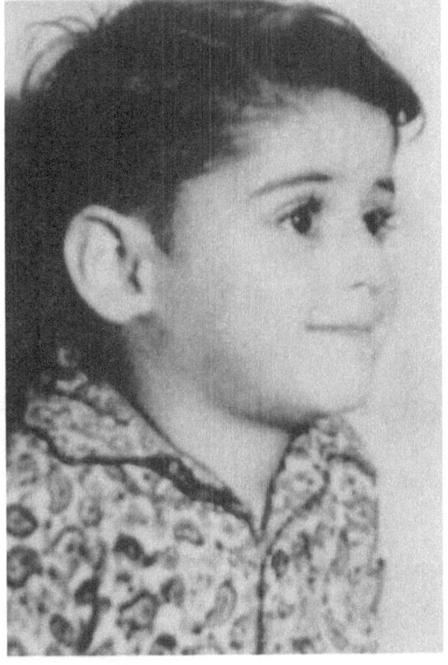

In our blissful life at Motamai cottage, two things brought the outside world to us. The radio and the newspaper.

We had not yet entered the world of miniatures. The radio was the size of a small suitcase, except that it did not travel anywhere. It sat in a corner of the living room on a wall-bracket six feet high. This was strange in a household where most people were less than six feet tall.

We listened to the radio for an hour or two in the evenings. This was a group activity, as if the cost of using electricity for the radio was best served if the news and programs reached more ears. Like trying to get maximum return on investment.

First a call would go around the house summoning everyone to the radio. Shouts would come from remote corners of the house: "Wait, wait, don't start," or "Don't switch it on. I don't want to miss anything." This made me think that there was someone hiding behind the radio who was performing for us on cue. Then, I got to thinking – how will this person run from house to house at the same time, and hide behind the radio without anyone seeing them?

"Where is that aunty speaking from?" I asked my uncle, one day.

He pointed to the electrical lines overhead and said, "From there."

For several days after that, when the adults were huddled on chairs or on the floor close to the radio, I went out of the house and looked at the electric lines, expecting to see miniature radio aunties and uncles sprinting in a tearing hurry on the electric lines to get behind the radio and talk from all the houses. But all I saw were crows cawing loudly.

On rare occasions, the radio would not work. Accusations would fly back and forth, everyone holding the other responsible for not renewing the radio license. After that there would be a frantic search for the license book. Everyone would swear that it was under the radio. A chair would be dragged close to the wall mounted radio. My tallest uncle would climb on it and lift the radio carefully. "There is only dust here," he would say.

Helpfully, someone would hand a dust cloth to him. "You

already climbed, na? Just wipe."

Someone else would try to crack a joke. "Who knows, maybe the license book is buried under all that dust."

My uncle would clamber down, sneeze a couple of times because of the dust, glare at everyone, and walk off without a word.

Eventually, the license book would be found on the book shelf, hiding between two books. Then, an argument would begin about who had to go to the post office to stand in a long, serpentine queue and renew the license.

Besides the radio, Hindi movies brought us a lot of excitement. The opening night of every new movie would be announced three to six months in advance. There was only one theatre close to us located between Vakola and Santacruz - Roop Talkies, which was built soon after the era of the silent movies.

Movie day arrived with gala festivities amid celebrations and lots of fanfare. The price of a ticket was four annas, or a quarter of a rupee. My sister Lily and I would get all excited and dressed up by 10 am for a 5 pm show, and spend the next 6 to 7 hours in excruciating impatience.

If anyone asked me what my uncles and aunts did all day, I would say they read newspapers. If the person asked me what work they did all day, I would again say they read newspapers. I thought that was their job, since they paid so much attention to it, squabbled over how long each one took to read, and had long and animated arguments over what was written in the newspaper.

Every day the newspaper vendor would bring The Times of India, Indian Express, Bombay Samachar and Gujarat Samachar. In fact, there were so many readers, that we got two copies of Times of India because my father took one copy with him to office. Once a week, the Parsi paper Jam-e-Jamshed would get delivered. Everyone paced to the front door and back, waiting for the newspapers, and welcomed its arrival like a much liked friend. On the days when the newspaper was not delivered, due to a festival or something, they scoured the previous day's newspapers, in case they had missed some crucial message.

My aunt, Perin maasi, decided to use this obsession with newspapers to play a prank on me. She was doubly related to me. She was my mother's youngest sister, and she was married to my father's younger brother Naval maasa. She loved us a lot and was like a second mother to us.

One day, she sidled up to me and whispered in my ear. "Do you know your dad has no job these days?" she said.

"Then where does he go every day?" I asked.

"He goes to sell chana-sing (grams and peanuts) at Santacruz railway station" she said.

"All lies. My daddy strongest!" I said at the top of my voice. "My daddy strongest!" was my war cry after my dad's courageous and fearless heroics in Shimla.

"Haven't you seen?" Perin maasi asked. "He carries a newspaper with him every morning."

"Yes, to read," I said.

She patted my head. "You poor child, don't know anything," she said. "Not to read. To wrap chana-sing for all the customers."

The next morning, I was heartbroken to see my dad walk out of the house with a folded newspaper in his hand, and return in the evening without the newspaper. Did he sell chana-sing until he ran out of paper or until he ran out of chana-sing? What happened to my courageous and fearless dad? I cried over this for several nights.

Perin maasi's pranks did not stop there.

Once she was peeling and feeding me a sweet orange. I swallowed an orange seed by mistake. When I told her about it, she exclaimed, "O God, big problem! Big, big problem!"

Then she leaned in and whispered into my ears that an orange tree would soon start growing in my stomach and come out of my ears. It might even grow out of my nose.

I was panic-stricken and refused to eat the rest of the orange. What if I swallowed another seed? Where would that tree grow out of? My mouth? How would I talk?

Perin maasi brought a huge torch and investigated my ears. She lit up my nostrils and my gaping mouth. She comforted me and said it would take a few days to grow. "Don't worry," she said. "When the branches started poking out, I will trim them for you. No one will know that you are now a tree-boy."

"What if it starts poking out in the night?" I asked.

Perin maasi looked at me admiringly as if I was a clever boy. She scrunched her face as if she was thinking. "I know," she said. "I will leave a pair of scissors or cutters under your pillow every night and take it away in the morning."

I was a nervous wreck! I had to be vigilant throughout the day and night and not poke myself in my sleep with the scissors. Why had I ever eaten the orange? Banana would have been better.

"But you are such a lucky boy," Perin maasi said. "Once the fruits start growing, no need to wait for me or mummy to give you oranges. You want one orange, pluck from the ears. You want one more orange, pluck from the nose."

For some time, I was happy with that thought. I could make lots of friends if they knew I could give them oranges on demand.

Every few hours, I went to the mirror and checked every cavity and every orifice on my face. At night I slept with a torch in my hand, underneath a double bedcover. I kept checking my nose and my ears all the time.

When I woke up the next morning, a dreadful thought came to my mind. "What if the orange tree grew from my bottom?" I squirmed. That would be painful. I could pretend that I was special and had grown a tail. But when it started sprouting oranges? What then?

My brother Rusi noticed that I was always looking into the mirror and digging into my nose and ears. "Stop digging for gold in your nose," Rusi said. "Where did you pick up this bad habit?"

"I am not digging for gold," I said. "I am digging for oranges."

"What?" he said.

The story came tumbling out. Rusi laughed for one whole day, I think. When he stopped laughing, he made me sit down and explained to me that the seed must have passed out of my body by then. "If you want, go and look in the barrel below the toilet cabin. Once you fell in. Now your orange seed fell in." I shuddered, but what immense relief I felt!

Such were the pranks and jest of my dearest Perin maasi. When I confronted her, she hugged me and held me tight, perhaps feeling guilty for pulling my leg.

But I was a gullible boy, and it was easy to play pranks on me.

My uncles used to clean and brush their teeth with well-cut sticks call 'daatoon' from a specific tree in the compound. All except Dhunjishaw uncle who would clean his teeth with tobacco powder—tapkeer—also known as snuff.

One morning, I was intently watching my uncle brushing his

teeth vigorously with tobacco powder. Noticing me, my uncle asked me if I wanted to try it, and held out his hand. I was always up for a challenge.

I was once challenged to eat three or four green chillies together. I took up the challenge and won the bet!

Unfortunately, in this case, instead of spitting out the tobacco powder after brushing, I made the mistake of swallowing it.

I became very dizzy, giddy, and sick for three days. From my bed, miserable and weak, I had the pleasure of hearing everyone scold Dhunjishaw uncle for giving tobacco powder to a six-year-old.

4

Aepiscopo's (mis)adventure

Finally it was time for us to leave my grandmother's Motamai cottage in Vakola. Six months after our arrival in Bombay, my father had rented an apartment in town. We moved to Nana Chowk, on Grant Road. By then, I was six years old and joined the second standard in The Cathedral & John Connon School in the Fort area.

I was very eager to start second standard. This was the year we could start using pens, and my father had bought me a brand-new Parker fountain pen. I was also excited about making friends in school. When I saw a European boy much bigger and a lot stronger than me sitting next to me in class, I was happy thinking he would protect me from big bullies. His name was Aepiscopo. He was a year older than me. Much later I came to know that he was the son of an ambassador from Europe.

Unfortunately, he turned out to be the biggest bully in my class and became a very tough oppressor. He harassed me and many others in the class all the time. He was a punk and a hooligan.

During recess, we used to gather in the playground and play with our marbles. When we saw Aepiscopo coming towards us, we grabbed our marbles, hid them and pretended to play something else. But he always picked on me. He would compel me to play marbles with him and snatch away most of my beautifully coloured glass marbles, even when I was winning.

I was determined not to part with my most favourite marble. It was a big, heavy, shining steel marble, like a mini steel ball which I called The Dom. If struck properly, The Dom would crack any glass marble to smithereens. It was my most prized possession and I hid it in my inside pocket.

I only took it out to play when Aepiscopo was not in the playground. But he must have seen the shape of a marble – one he had not yet usurped from me – in my pocket. He held me by force and reached in and pulled out The Dom. I was furious and angry that I did not have the strength to fight back, but I vowed to get even with him. I waited for a chance.

In class after recess, Aepiscopo stood up to answer a question asked by Miss Daniel, our class teacher. In a flash, I removed the cap of my Parker fountain pen and held it erect, exactly under his bum. In my excitement, I did not stop to consider the damage it would do – both to his bum and the nib of my pen.

The boys behind me sucked in their breath. They saw how I planned to extract revenge. Aepiscopo sat down with a thump directly on top of the open pen. The nib went through his bottom. He screamed and screamed. I yanked the pen out, but it did not come out. There was blood all over his pants; his bottom and my hand were covered in blood. I removed my hand, but the pen was still stuck inside.

The Parsi Lying-in Hospital was across the road from our school. I had been born in that hospital. Even though we lived in Shimla, my mother had come to Bombay to give birth to me. The Parsi Lying-in Hospital was meant only for Parsis, but I was surprised to see Aepiscopo being rushed there for immediate first aid and stitches.

I was in big trouble. My father and Aepiscopo's father were summoned urgently. Aepiscopo's father, being an ambassador from Europe, had a lot of clout. I thought I would be suspended from school. But my other classmates began chattering like magpies. Aepiscopo was a big bully and a tormentor to boys smaller than him. They added their voice to mine when questioned by the principal and Miss Daniel, and Aepiscopo's bullying was out in the open. I was given a severe warning and suspended from school for three days as punishment.

"I bought you a new pen to write, not to push into someone's bum," my father grumbled, and bought me a new nib for my pen.

When I returned to school after three days, I was given a hero's welcome. I had taught Aepiscopo a lesson he would never forget.

Aepiscopo too returned to school after three days. Nobody feared him anymore. Whenever he saw me, he turned tail and ran in the other direction.

I was the new leader of the class. I had no intention of forming a gang, or becoming a gang leader, but my little class buddies always walked with and around me, shoulder to shoulder—and Aepiscopo stayed far away from us.

5

National Anthem at Midnight

When I watch and listen to debates raging about national and regional languages, I am taken back to the days when one was neither seen nor heard.

My father was the Collector of Customs & Central Excise, and we lived in a vast bungalow, with the nameboard 'Nawab's Bungalow' when he was posted in Ahmedabad. Along with his job title, we also had three or four sepoys to take care of the family and the bungalow. We called them orderlies and they were at our beck & call. I have always wondered about the origin of that word – was it because we could order them around? We even had a special attendant just to fan us during the hot months of summer in Ahmedabad.

Needless to say, I felt like a young Nawab, a Prince, in my teens.

But the world outside of my cossetted life was undergoing a change that would affect me.

The bilingual state of Bombay had a Marathi and Gujarati speaking population. The Mahagujarat movement, known locally as the Mahagujarat Andolan, was gaining momentum. It was a political movement demanding a separate state for Gujarati speaking people – to be called Gujarat.

The Government of India saw trouble simmering in the

bilingual state of Bombay and passed a reorganizing act in Parliament on 1st May 1960. The two populations were bifurcated: the Gujarati speaking people formed the State of Gujarat, and the Maharashtrians, the State of Maharashtra. Both states attained new statehood.

I was studying in Ahmedabad at that time, which ended up falling in Gujarat. It was rumored that colleges and Universities of Ahmedabad, Baroda, Anand, etc., would switch over from teaching in English to Gujarati. All of a sudden, English became the forbidden fruit in Gujarat. As it is, my Bombaiyya Parsi-Bawa-Gujarati was an ongoing joke among my peers. Switching to Gujarati as a medium of studies, became a nightmare for me and my parents.

Out of the blue, I was yanked out of my life of opulence and luxury from Nawab's Bungalow in the city of Amdavad (as we called it; and, the city I had grown to love) and moved to Bombay.

I dearly missed my life in Ahmedabad, my Parsi Gymkhana by the Sabarmati River. I missed my close friends and mostly, my parents. But my brother Rusi worked with Air India in Bombay. His family made up for my sudden, abrupt and unforeseen separation. But there was also the added worry of getting an admission into a good college in Bombay, which were filling up fast. To my advantage, I had won an All Parsi Open Chess Championship in Ahmedabad at the age of fourteen. That became the ace in my cap and St. Xaviers College welcomed me eagerly on the 'sports' quota.

Rusi lived in a one-bedroom house on Sleater Road opposite Grant Road railway station, with his wife, Gover and his three children. Also, before I forget, a live-in maid. Enter the younger brother from Ahmedabad. Rusi and Gover's hearts were several times the size of their apartment and they welcomed me with open arms and hearts.

In homes where even the goldfish has its own room, it is hard to think of so many people in a one-bedroom house. But it's floor to ceiling French windows in the living and dining rooms made it feel expansive and large. In the night, the living room doubled as a bedroom for Rusi's family. They spread out on a massive king-sized bed, including the three children. The dining room doubled as my bedroom. I had a small but cozy single bed. If memory serves me right, the maid slept in the kitchen or maybe the pantry. It was like living in a fishbowl, but we never felt like goldfish.

I stayed with my brother through the three years of college, and even after I got a job midway through my last term of college. In November 1962, I got a job as a junior cargo assistant (JCA) in Air India.

A year later, I heard that an old retired Parsi gentleman, Mr. Khurshedji Lala and his wife Dinamai, living in Cusrow Baug, were looking to lease out one of their rooms to a young, reliable Parsi boy or girl, with emphasis on the word 'reliable' and 'dependable.' I jumped at the offer; and, to them, I fit the bill. Those days, I earned about Rs. 250-300 per month and hoped the rent would not be too high. But they won my heart (and my purse) by saying they would accept whatever I could afford.

Dinamai and Khurshedji Lala were the nicest couple I had ever met and lived with. I also found several ways to get involved in their life and return their hospitality.

Once on Dinamai's birthday, I pulled Khurshedji into planning a surprise party for her. I brought 3 mawa cupcakes, 3 small candles and a bouquet of roses. Even more excited than Dinamai was Khurshedji. He was overjoyed that he was part of a surprise birthday. In an Air India envelope, I placed one Rs. 10 note and a Rs. 1 coin to gift Dinamai. Those days, Rs. 11 in an envelope with kumkum (Vermillion) on it, was an auspicious gift. The return smile from Dinamai was worth a million.

In return, when my birthday rolled around on the 18th of December, Dinamai added another Rs. 10 note in a fresh envelope to make up Rs. 21, with extra dark red kumkum and gifted it (a peramni) to me for good luck.

For Khurshedji's birthday, I planned a different surprise. He had a small defect from birth. His one leg was shorter by a few inches than the other. He had to wear specially designed shoes, with one heel four inches higher than the other.

On his birthday, I snuck his brown leather shoes in a cloth bag and took it to a shoe-shine boy across the street. I told him to give it an extra-extra special sheen and shimmer, sparkle and luster with imported cream polish. He also got into the act and gave it his saliva treatment on the leather to enhance the glow. No, he did not lick the shoes. It was common practice to spit on the leather.

Looking at his spit-spot shoes on his birthday, Khurshedji became very emotional and his eyes brimmed over. As did mine.

I learnt that day, that doing 'little' things for people brought the most happiness, both to the giver and the receiver.

While on the subject of Khurshedji's shoes, with Dinamai it was always how you looked at things. In an unrelated argument with her neighbour, Mrs Ayee Mai, the neighbour brought Khurshedji into the fight by saying, "Havay jaa-jaa-jaa, as it is your husband's one leg is short." Not to be outdone, Dinamai shouted back saying, "Aye, Ayee Mai, my husband's one leg is LONGER than the other."

She was obsessively protective of people she considered her own, even the dead. Every day, Dinamai would read the obituaries in the Parsi paper, 'Jam-e-Jamshed' and underline the names of the departed whether she knew them or not. She noted down their funeral times at the Parsi Dokhma (funeral home) at Kemps Corner. She would adorn her white sari and blouse, drape a head scarf to cover her head and leave the house. Even though she was more than sixty years old, she would take a bus from Colaba Causeway to Kemps corner. She would buy some sandalwood at the Doongarwadi Gate, and begin her climb uphill, towards the Parsi Tower of Silence. She would then systematically visit all the different 'bunglees' (individual prayer halls) and kneel to the departed souls as a mark of respect for their last rites. Only a righteous, pious and humane person like Dinamai would have it in her to perform this social duty.

After such a day, I would secretly take Dinamai's white sari and blouse to the laundry opposite Cusrow Baug and have them whitened and dry cleaned. I would leave the laundry bag on her bed as my mark of respect and gratitude for what she did for the departed souls.

I now come to another reason why I loved staying with Dinamai and Khurshedji. My 'one sided girlfriend' Maloo lived in the building alongside this one and on the same floor. One sided because only I, Me, and Myself was having a love affair with Maloo, in my own mind. I knew Maloo because her aunt, Gover, was married to my brother, Rusi. So, she was no stranger. In Cusrow Baug, I would loiter on the third-floor balcony to catch a glimpse of my captivating love. When she saw me, we signaled back and forth in sign language, but it was quite unromantic because she did not know that I yearned for her love. To her, we were friends.

Maloo took part in some outings with Dinamai and Khurshedji. Once, we took them to the Royal Circus in Azad Maidan, but Dinamai made us leave after feeding the elephants a bunch of bananas and banana leaves and watching the clown show. She did not want to watch the Daredevil motorcycle riders in the Wheel of Death. "Come on, come on, get up, get up, let's go, let's go," she urged everyone and headed out. We had no choice but to follow her like the performers walking behind the ring master. No one could change her mind.

Dinamai and Khurshedji always called me 'dikra' (son), and that is how I felt. Whenever I went to Ahmedabad, I felt like I was going from one parents' house to another. Home was at both ends. On these trips, Dinamai packed some omelet sandwiches, and 'Vasanoo', a Parsi delicacy to be enjoyed on the train ride. On my return, I always brought back gifts: one white saree and blouse piece for Dinamai, and one very colorful, flowery Hawaiian shirt for Khurshedji. He was so fond of those shirts that every now and then he hinted that I should go and visit my parents. "They must be missing you," he said.

Of course, I also brought back a few, very vivid and multicolored 'Bandhani' sarees (a specialty of Rajasthan and Gujarat) for Maloo.

Those were the days of listening to radios and every night, Dinamai would play lilting, melodious Hindi film songs on the 'Geetmala' program on her radio. Khurshedji would be lulled into a cozy slumber, nodding off by her side.

By midnight, the program ended, and the radio station would sign off by playing the national anthem. Dinamai stood up in respect for the national anthem. Then realizing that uncle was sleeping, she would wake him, shake him and spur him into a standing position, half asleep. How he managed to stay upright while sleeping, is one of life's mysteries. At the end of the national anthem, Dinamai would give him a gentle nudge and a soft push. Khurshedji would be back in his horizontal position on the bed. This happened every single night during all the years that I lived with them.

They were my surrogate parents.

In case, the readers are wondering what happened to the one-sided love affair: when I finally popped the question, it took Maloo less than ten seconds to say "Yes"!

6

Honesty is the Best Policy

When you are in love, you live in the clouds and spend your time with the love of your life in the various rooms that you have built together in the clouds. Only when the wedding date peeps through the clouds, do you come down to earth with a thud.

I had applied for a rental apartment from my employers and was put on a waiting list in the Air India staff quarters in Kalina, Santacruz East.

A few months before our wedding (11th February 1966), Sharan Penang, my friend and colleague in Air India traffic department, agreed to rent me his one-bedroom apartment on Cadell Road, close to Shivaji Park in Bombay. Back in the day, we did not have multi-page rental agreements. Oral agreements were binding. Trust was everything. I paid him six months rent as a term deposit, and another one month's rent in advance.

Satisfied that I had done everything to offer my new bride a roof over her head, my beautiful newly-wed wife Meherangiz (more popularly known as Maloo, and Manan by our first grandchild Kaizia) and I left on our honeymoon to a hill resort, Mt. Abu. Sharan Penang was going to get the apartment painted before I returned. He promised to leave the keys to the apartment with my brother Rusi after the painting was done.

We honeymooned at Hotel on the Hill in Mt. Abu But for us, it was Hotel in the Clouds. We slept with the windows open and would wake up in the morning with misty, frosty, and feathery white clouds drifting through our room. We were in the clouds, both literally and figuratively!

When we returned to Bombay, my brother Rusi was supposed to meet us at Bombay Central Station with the keys to the newly painted apartment on Cadell Road. Rusi was at the station. But no keys. While we were in the Hotel in the Clouds, Sharan Penang had sold the apartment! He was offered a good price for the apartment, and the deal was done. Sharan had returned the deposit and the advance rent.

So much for oral agreements! That was a hard lesson learnt!

We were dejected, despondent, and morose. After our glorious honeymoon, this was a sad homecoming. My parents lived in Ahmedabad. So, we couldn't live with them. Rusi took us to his house on Sleater Road. Rusi's wife, my sister-in-law Gover (who is also my wife Maloo's aunt) made us feel most welcome, and we settled down temporarily in my brother's place.

When I returned to my job in Air India Traffic, Santacruz, Sharan Penang was most apologetic and regretted letting me down. With great bravado and aplomb, I told him that had I known he was willing to sell his place, I would have topped the buyer's price with cash on the table. That made Sharan feel guilty and more miserable, but it made me happy to see him wallow in his guilt. Little did he know that was a bluff on my part—I could barely afford the advance rent of six months.

I have always believed that when one door closes, another one opens. Rusi's old friend, Shapoor Irani, who was settled in London, owned an apartment in Maganlal Nagar, Charni

Road Junction, Bombay. It was vacant and he was happy to rent his apartment to us on 'caretaker' basis. He wanted us to deposit a fixed amount in cash every month as rent to his old uncle, Minocher Irani, who worked in Chartered Bank in Fort area. Just like that, we had a furnished two room, kitchen, and balcony apartment! We stayed there for over a year. Zeena, our first child was born there.

Unfortunately, our dear friend Shapoor met with a serious and fatal car accident in London. He was a bachelor with no relatives, successors, or claimants to his apartment in Bombay. We were now caretakers for an orphaned apartment. Minocher Irani told me that since his nephew Shapoor had made us the caretakers of his apartment in Bombay, the apartment was ours for keeps. For keeps? How could I do that? I was an unrelated third party.

Meanwhile, my name had worked its way up the waitlist and I was allotted a one-bedroom flat in Air India Staff Colony, Santacruz, Bombay. I now had the keys to Flat Number 6, Building Number 17, along with the keys to Shapoor's apartment in Maganlal Nagar, to boot. Shapoor's uncle had retired and was in poor health. He did not want anything to do with the keys or his nephew's apartment. He kept insisting I was the legal caretaker, and it was mine!

I could have kept the Maganlal Nagar house forever! However, being a Parsi, such thoughts did not enter my mind. Finally, after much persuasion, Minocherji reluctantly accepted the keys from me.

In these avaricious days of real estate greed, I am sure many of my readers will be shaking their heads at my naivete and insistence on doing the right thing. But I have never wanted anything that I did not earn myself, and I live a happy and contented life.

7

Air India Training School Days

Some of us take so many things for granted in our upbringing: an English language education, and exposure to lives outside of our homes and our place of birth. But when you meet someone who has not had the same exposure, your encounters humble you and give you an appreciation and respect for all mankind.

It was the same with Harbhajan Motta, most lovingly called Bhajji – my batchmate during Air India training. He was a Sardar, in his early twenties, a wonderful and simple human being. Until I met him, I did not know that there are cities where English is rarely spoken. Bhajji told me that in Chandigarh everyone spoke to the other in Punjabi. No one ever spoke in English, like they do in Bombay and especially in Air India, he said. He confessed that when he spoke in English, he would first think in Punjabi, and then translate it into English.

But I am jumping ahead. Let me rewind to my start with Air India.

On 20th November 1962, I joined Air India as a Junior Cargo Assistant (JCA) attending to Air India cargo. After a year, I was promoted to a Senior Traffic Assistant (STA) and transferred to the Air India traffic section, handling passengers.

A few years later, in March 1968, I was close to being promoted to Chief Traffic Assistant (CTA). At the same time, I was selected for a flying job as an Assistant Flight Purser (AFP) in Air India in-flight service department. With two career tracks in hand, friends and colleagues would kid me, "Aap tau bade Saheb bun gaye!" (Now you have become a big shot!) If only they knew! The move was actually a double demotion, of sorts. But I took it because as a flying crew member, I could look forward to a great life for my family, with the opportunity to travel to international destinations.

With the new posting, I started a three-month training in March 1968 in the in-flight service department, along with sixteen other batchmates. Bhajji was one of my batchmates. With six years of experience on the ground in Air India, I was the monitor of the class, and we formed a very close bond. Even today, after more than half a century, we still keep in touch with each other, except for the ones who have moved on to fly even higher – to their heavenly abode.

During our training, we also got some unofficial training which was in none of the training manuals, but we were told to accept it (with a smile) as a 'fact of life.' It was: "The in-flight supervisor kicks the senior check flight purser. The senior check flight kicks the flight purser. The flight purser kicks the assistant flight purser, and the assistant flight purser, not to be outdone, kicks the fridge door in the galley."

Back to Bhajji.

He had written a letter to his father which went like this:

Respected and honoured Pappaji,

I am well, and I hope you are in the same well. I am hopping you and Mammaji are in full swings in Chandigarh. I am also in the pinks of health.

Our training for flying is in advance motion. Our teacher

is saying, when we fly, we will become ambassadors of our country when we go to foreign.

I think this is a government job.

Best wishes and respect,

Harbhajan Motta. BA. LLB.

Bhajji asked me if the letter was okay or if it required any minor changes. By then, he had already told me about how people in Chandigarh were not like people in Bombay, who spoke English with ease. So, I told him it was good. He looked at me very skeptically. I explained that the closing of the letter need not have his educational qualifications after his name, especially since he was writing to his father, and it was a personal letter.

He looked shocked. How could he omit his degree after his name? Pappaji had taken all the trouble and struggled hard so that Bhajji could get a BA. LLB and a government job. It was particularly important and essential to put BA. LLB in a letter to pappaji. It showed gratitude and respect. Even to a jolly fellow like me, his words made me choke up. I told him his letter was fine and ready to post. Harbhajan Motta was incredibly happy to get my approval. He did not know that he taught me a lesson in gratitude.

But no exposure to lives outside of his home and place of birth did trip up Bhajji a lot during our training.

Our in-flight service training centre had four separate classrooms for the theory classes. The rest of the training centre was designed like the interior of a Boeing 707. The galleys were identical to the ones on board a real aircraft. The seats between the two galleys were first class seats. The front of the cabin was a mock-up of the first-class galley, and the rear was a mock-up for the economy-class galley. Both the galleys were designed for the 'hands-on' practical part of our training. We were split into groups of three and four crew members to conduct regular meal services (dry runs and otherwise) both in the first class and economy class.

As AFP's we were expected to be one step ahead at all times during the service. We were required to keep everything readily available and in specific locations for the flight purser and airhostesses. During one such run, Bhajji was working in the front galley. Our instructor, assistant chief airhostess, Ms. Champa Malkhani was supervising the proceedings from the other end. The curtain between the galley and the cabin was half drawn and Ms. Malkhani could not see what Bhajji was doing in the galley. She asked Bhajji to draw the curtain so she could observe properly. Harbhajan was supposed to prepare the first-class galley with everything in readiness, for the meal service. His job was to do a proper 'mis en place' before the service. He was very confused and, instead of opening the curtain fully, he closed it fully, causing Ms. Malkhani to cluck in annoyance.

During the service, every individual item of crockery and cutlery for the first-class passengers had to be placed in the correct sequence on their drop table tops. It was termed as 'table setting'. Every item, like wine glasses, bread plates, cutlery, salt, and pepper shakers had very specific placements on the table layout. Some senior staff members of other departments were often invited to lunch in the first-class cabin, while the trainees conducted an actual hot meal service.

Bhajji had set the tray tables for two passengers. However, his settings were a disaster. Every item was placed willy-nilly on the passenger's drop table, as if he thought they would find it if they really needed it. Out of the fourteen items to be set, eight were in the wrong place. Ms. Malkhani was calm and patient. She asked Bhajji if he noticed anything wrong in the table setting. Bhajji pondered very intently, and attentively observed the table. "The centaur is not facing the pussanger," he said. Turning it around to face the passenger, Bhajji stepped back and beamed at Ms. Malkhani.

Ms. Malkhani was stupefied and speechless. Bhajji pronounced passenger as "pussanger". The Sagittarian centaur, etched on every individual crystal glass, was to be set with the centaur facing the passenger. She could not believe that with everything on the table being misplaced, Harbhajan had found the smallest of the mistakes, and not the others. The invitees and the class broke into giggles. Bhajji was a good sport. He laughed at himself, too.

The next day, Bhajji reached the training centre late, while the class was in progress. Chief Flight Purser (CFP) Mr. Lorry Noronha was teaching the class. Bhajji was in his chappals with one big toe in bandages. Shoes with laces and neckties were mandatory during training, but Bhajji had an explanation for his chappals. "My left leg thumb is injured and hurting," he said. Mr. Noronha very sympathetically explained that the thumb is on the hand, and the toe is on the foot! Bhajji thanked him and hobbled to his seat.

After three months of training, everyone had to go on a couple of trainee flights to observe and learn. After each trainee flight, the flight purser in charge gave an appraisal and assessment report, which we had to show the chief flight purser, Mr. Noronha. He would check our progress to see if we could be cleared to fly solo. Most of us would do maybe two or three flights as trainees before we were released to fly solo.

However, Bhajji had already done seven trainee short and 'quick-turn-around' flights and still had not been released to fly solo. Mr. Noronha decided that he should go back to the training school and join a fresh batch of trainees who were already two weeks into training.

Bhajji was anxious and worried that he would be two weeks late. "How will I catch up with the new batch?" he asked.

Mr. Noronha almost fainted. "Catch up? You have already done this training. You should be in a position to train those trainees," he said, trying his best not to laugh.

Bhajji thought he was a fresh trainee and had not realized that he had already attended a full three-month training course and done seven return flights.

We lost touch after he went back into training, but I bumped into him months later in Beirut. He was shopping in a clothing store in a terribly busy marketplace called Change Alley. I asked him how he was and what was he doing in Change Alley. "I'm buying some cold clothes for the warm weather in Bombay," he said. I was clueless how to respond but was immediately left scratching my head when he complained that the hotel bathroom had an exceptionally low second basin, with a waterspout to wash his face. I took a couple of steps back, realizing that he was referring to the bidet next to the toilet seat! I scooted out of there, with that picture in my mind.

These were the innocent gaffes of Harbhajan Motta. He managed to survive every new experience in his own way. He never spoke ill of others. He always showed interest in others, and readily apologized for any mistakes he had made. He was honest, frank, kind, gentle, and humble.

I loved him for his simplicity and his naturalness.

8

My First Solo Flight

It is strange to write this in the aftermath of the #MeToo movement, but it will serve well in drawing a comparison between the late 60s and the current era. Some of us were staunch allies and supporters of the movement before it was even born. Before it even had a name. Before the term sexual harassment became part of our vocabulary.

I had finished three months of training as an Assistant Flight Purser (AFP) for Air India in June 1968 and was accepted as a regular AFP, rostered on the weekly cabin crew flight program. After two trainee flights I was finally on my very first solo flight to Beirut, Lebanon and back to Bombay after a two-day layover in Beirut.

In the very early Boeing 707 days, we flew with a team of seven cabin crew on board. Our flight to Beirut had two very senior flight pursers, Ashwin Bhandarkar and Kishan Puri, Freddy Gadekar, my very junior batchmate on his second solo flight, and three very junior, rookie airhostesses, Cynthia Thomas, Asha Thelma, and Bina.

After our arrival and check-in at hotel La Commodore in Beirut, the senior flight pursers, Ashwin and Kishan, instructed the three airhostesses to get dressed for an evening out and join them in the lobby in one hour for drinks.

Asked where they were going, Ashwin mentioned the name of the night club in the basement of the very same hotel. For all the attention they gave us, Freddy Gadekar and I might as well have been the potted plants placed in the corner of the lobby. We were not invited. However, as guests of the hotel, when we checked in, we were all given free, one-time entrance tickets to the nightclub, plus coupons for two free welcome drinks each. So, we really didn't need an invitation.

A while later, the young ladies knocked softly on Freddy's room door, and from there summoned me from my room. "Don't let Ashwin or Kishan see you coming in here," Bina whispered. What clandestine activities were they planning? I opened my room door and scuttled into Freddy's room.

The young ladies did not want to go to the night club.

"So, don't go," I said.

They looked at me like I was a rookie and couldn't imagine how I had been released to fly solo.

Freddy was more worldly wise than me. "Say you have a headache," he said.

Now they looked at Freddy as if they had to send him back to training again. "All three of us? A headache at the same time?" Asha asked.

We, the two clueless men in the room, nodded our heads solemnly in unison. "Ah, you have a point," I said. "Maybe two of you can go and one person can pretend to have a headache."

"And how to decide who has a headache?" Cynthia asked. "Do a coin toss?"

I realized we were giving all three of them a headache with our unhelpful suggestions. Finally, it dawned on us that they were asking us to come with them to the night club as chaperones. Both the senior flight pursers had been pushy and assertive and had been hitting on the three airhostesses all through the flight.

"But they didn't invite us," Freddy said.

"Don't worry," I said. "We will escort you to the night club." I threw on my invisible cloak of chivalry.

"But…," Freddy said.

"We have our own entrance tickets and drink coupons, Freddy," I reminded him sternly.

An hour later, we were all in the hotel lobby. Ashwin and Kishan did a double take when they saw five instead of three people coming down together, but they did not object, since they didn't expect two junior lackeys to cramp their style.

The night club was a dark smoke-filled tavern, heavy with loud disco beats. A cabaret show was in progress on the stage as we entered.

Ashwin Bhandarkar had only reserved a table for five, but undaunted, I managed to get the waiters join one more table for all of us. Ashwin and Kishan glowered at me, but nothing could pierce my cloak of chivalry. We ordered our drinks, but before we could settle in, the senior flight pursers took two of the airhostesses onto the dancing floor. Like an expert sleuth, Freddy asked Bina to dance with him, so that they could keep an eye on 'those two buggers.'

I sat there, enjoying the music, sipping my Bloody Mary, and making smoke rings in the air, thinking Freddy had it all under control. They came back every now and then to replenish their drinks. After an hour or so, Bina and Asha whispered to me and Freddy that Ashwin and Kishan were getting a bit rash and being objectionable – crossing the line, as we called it those days. When Ashwin and Kishan swayed back to the table and ordered two more doubles of Black

Label, probably their sixth or seventh drink, Bina stood up abruptly, excused herself, and left. I signaled to Freddy to accompany her, in case, the obnoxious guys decided to coerce her to stay.

Cynthia and Asha said that they were exhausted and would also be retiring for the night. This seemed like waving a red flag before Ashwin and he was getting a little unmanageable - drunk and rowdy. I got up with them and repeated firmly, but politely that we were going up to our rooms.

"Sit!" Ashwin ordered.

I stopped and looked around me.

"What are you looking at?" he bellowed.

"For your pet dog to follow your command," I said. "Don't order me around. We are not on duty." With that, the three of us signed our individual room numbers and left the night club, ignoring Ashwin.

Cynthia and Asha decided to stay together in one room for the night, expecting more rowdy and belligerent behaviour from the two senior flight pursers.

I got ready for bed, and was turning back the covers, when I heard a huge commotion in the corridor. At first, I ignored it, but when it continued, curiosity got the better of me. I cracked open my door a couple of inches and was appalled at the sight in the corridor between the rooms.

Kishan had discarded all his clothes and was stomping around in a skimpy towel wrapped around his huge potbelly. I did not know how long it would be before the towel gave up the battle with the potbelly and slid (un)gracefully to the ground.

They were both running up and down the corridor, completely blown out of their minds after all those drinks, shouting, singing loudly and off-key.

The lyrics were:

Noshir is a bastard!

Noshir is a bastard!!

On repeat.

All they had to do was kick their legs in the air, and I could call the three young ladies and Freddy to watch our own private cabaret show. But I had had enough of these macho antics for the night. I closed my door.

But they were still on a roll. Way past midnight, they started knocking and banging on my door. I called the front desk, gave them my room number, and told them of the commotion on my floor. Ten minutes later, everything was quiet again. The security staff must have urged our singers to go back into their rooms.

But my night was not done. The phone rang. It was Cynthia and Asha inquiring if I was okay. I told them their harassers were now after me and they could go back to sleep. I suspect I heard a giggle from their end. "Call us if you need help," they said. I hung up on them.

Two minutes later, Freddy called. He too had heard the abuses thrown at me in the corridor. I told Freddy everything was cool, and could he please let me go to sleep?

The next morning, Ashwin and Kishan were missing at the breakfast buffet table. They were probably out for the count. The five of us hoped they would not remember anything that happened the previous night when they were sloshed. But our hopes were dashed. I had now become the victim.

Ashwin called me at 4:00 pm to his room. Ashwin and Kishan were both having their first morning cup of tea. At 4:00 pm They offered me a cup of tea, but I declined politely. I knew they were fattening me up for the kill.

"I know this is your first solo flight," Ashwin said.

"And it is also your last," Kishan said.

"After landing in Bombay, only one of us will be in Air India," Ashwin said, "and it won't be you."

I didn't offer any apology.

"Who the hell do you think you are, anyway? J.R.D Tata's son?" Kishan said.

They continued in this vein for a few minutes, until I got up and walked out of the room, slamming the door behind me. It took me a while to calm down, with Freddy trying to console me and the ladies blaming themselves for getting me into this mess. I decided I would take up this challenge. I had confidence that Air India was not the mafia, and the mob wasn't running it.

When we gathered in the lobby the next day for the pick-up for our flight, I wondered how I would deal with the threatening duo until touch down in Bombay. When Ashwin came towards me in the hotel lobby, I got ready for a punch and clenched my fists for a return jab. To my surprise, he extended his hand towards me, patted me on the back and said, "Noshir, I'm sorry. Let's forget these last two days. I was wrong," while the crew stood around and gaped at this 360-degree turn. I extended my hand, and we shook on it. Kishan Puri apologized to me on the flight. We continued homeward leaving all hard feelings back in Beirut.

As I write this, I wonder if they apologised to the three ladies for their behaviour. Today, I wish I had asked them, and if they had not, I wish I had brokered an apology between them and our three wonderful airhostesses.

To be honest, I knew those threats could not touch my career.

I have always had trust and faith in justice.

In the previous four months in the In-flight service department, I had won the hearts and 'goodwill' of all those who really mattered and all those that counted in the IFS department and in the airline.

My elder brother, Rusi was a Flight Purser in Air India before he chose to take up a ground job in Air India. During his flying days, he was very close to all my present bosses in the In-flight service department. Chief flight purser Mr. Lorry Noronha, deputy chief flight pursers Mr. Jimmy Naigamwala, Mr. Jal Khambatta and Mr. Melville D'Souza, chief airhostess Ms. Julie Dunn and deputy chiefs Ms. Collin Bhiwandiwalla and Ms. Champa Malkhani, were the senior most officers in the In-flight service department who knew the character of the two Sanjana brothers. If I ran into any of them, they would always ask me, "How is your brother Rusi?" to which I would reply, "He is well, but how come you never want to know how I am doing?"

9

The Exorcist Experience

In America, the day after Christmas is called – the day after Christmas! Or 26th December. But in Britain and all the other ex-British colonies, it is called Boxing Day, and is a holiday. I won't go into the origins of the name 'Boxing Day', but on the day after Christmas, one expects people to be relaxing after the revelries, or seated on a flight back home after visiting family for Christmas. Unless you happen to be the cabin crew flying for Air India, in which case you are not on a flight back to your family. You have landed in the vacation capital of the world – New York City(!) and are bitten by the first day first show bug.

No one expects to be seeing the horror films of all times on the day after Christmas. Where is Joy to the World and all that? I cannot fathom what made the producers of the film The Exorcist release it on 26th December, 1973 the world over. Who made that decision – let's release a movie of a young girl possessed by an evil spirit - on the day after Christmas?

My brother-in-law Carl, his wife Margarette, and I had operated a flight from London to New York. After reaching the crew hotel, Lexington, the three of us threw off our uniform, grabbed some regular clothes, put on our winter coats, and flagged down a taxi. Straight to the cinema hall -

first day, first show viewing of The Exorcist. After all the pre-release hype of this movie, we wanted bragging rights that we had seen it in New York.

It was the last week of December, and we were prepared for snow, but rain was pouring heavily when we reached the theatre. We jumped out of the taxi and hurried to buy our tickets. We kept walking... and walking... and walking to find the end of the line waiting to buy tickets. The line had stretched around the block. The tickets would be all sold out by the time we snaked our way to the ticket window.

In true Indian style, I thought the only chance we had to watch the movie that day would be to bribe our way in. The theatre doorman stood in his red velvety uniform in full glory at the door. I waved a $10 bill before Carl and asked him to try his magic with the doorman. Carl had the reputation of achieving the unthinkable and never walked away from a challenge.

Carl slipped out of the line and walked nonchalantly towards the doorman. He held the folded $10 bill discreetly in his palm and tried to strike up a conversation with the doorman. "We've come all the way from London to see this movie," he said, and extended his hand for a handshake. Shrewdly and confidently, by a sleight of hand, he showed the half-hidden $10 bill to the doorman and said very softly with a slight wink, "I have something for you."

The big guy saw the $10 bill and said, in a booming voice, "Hey Rockefeller! The only way you can see the movie tonight is by joining the end of that line!"

Carl suddenly wished he was ten feet underground and hurried back to join us in the queue. We stood in line in the pouring rain, our spirits as damp as our bodies. The line inched forward, and after thirty minutes, to our great surprise and delight, we got the last three tickets. Our elation soon turned to disappointment when we were ushered into the auditorium, and realized we were sitting right at the end of the very first row. We had the worst three seats in the entire auditorium.

The movie had already begun. When we settled down and got accustomed to the darkness, we found the huge screen right in our faces. To look at the screen, we had to lean back as far as the seat would allow and turn our necks from the extreme right seats towards the middle of the screen.

The Exorcist was an eerie, terrifying, and brutal horror movie. The film got more and more horrifying and scary, reel by reel. The horror was atmospheric, creating an ambience of pure suspenseful terror that preys on the rampant and vicious, prevailing human fears.

Linda Blair as Regan played the role of a sweet, twelve-year-old girl who goes through spells of bizarre behaviour patterns, possessed by an evil spirit—maybe the devil himself.

There are scenes in the film where Regan rotates her head a hundred and eighty degrees – somewhat like us from our extreme right front row seats. She regurgitates, ejects and pukes out horrendous green vomit. She levitates, floats and hovers high above her bed. Her voice, her utterances during her evil possession are the most gruff, thick, rasping, and guttural sounds anyone has ever heard.

Regan's distressed and deeply disturbed actress mother calls for a Catholic priest who recommends exorcism. The priest goes on to perform the exorcism at the risk to his own life.

The next two hours were the scariest two hours of our lives. For most of the movie, Margarette's eyes were shut tight. Yet, only listening to the background score and the sound effects, she had drawn blood from Carl's arms and mine. She clawed and scratched deep scars into us with her long nails. We kept trying to convince her that it was only a movie. Carl hugged his wife and held her tight to make her feel warm and safe. I wrapped my overcoat around her to add to the warmth.

The movie was still running when Margarette said she was feeling queasy. She was nauseous and wanted to throw up. She was cold and quite shaken. Carl checked her pulse rate. It was high, quite high. She was frozen to her seat. We could not get her to move. Margarette was having a panic attack!

On screen, the movie was coming to its climatic end. We had become a bit of a nuisance to the audience, by blocking their view. They had no idea what was happening and were loud and rude in their objections. "To hell with your movie. We have a medical emergency here," I shouted, but it was impossible to be heard above the deafening background score. People craned their necks around us to continue watching the movie. I realized the exorcism held them enthralled.

Some kind soul from the audience, not devoured by the evil spirit on the screen, offered Carl a bottle of water for Margarette. I rushed out of the auditorium and told the theatre usher that there was a medical emergency inside. Within minutes, a medic in a white coat and a nurse rushed into the auditorium with me. They checked Margarette's pulse, heartbeat, and her blood pressure, and placed two tablets under her tongue. They also gave her an injection. A wheelchair was rolled in, and she was moved to it. The three of us were out of the auditorium and in the theatre lobby within minutes. Everything was fine. Margarette had just averted a major panic attack.

By this time, the movie ended, and people started streaming out, staring curiously at our trio.

By then, Margarette had recovered. She was very, very

apologetic, and overly repentant. She vowed to never ever watch another horror movie in her life ever again. Inwardly, I promised myself never to go to the movies with Carl and Margarette ever again. At least not a horror movie unless I was willing to miss the ending.

On our way out, we saw that the theatre had arranged to park a couple of emergency ambulances and medical staff right across the street, in readiness for emergencies from *The Exorcist.*

Later we heard that the censor board introduced some additional cuts in the movie after the first week of viewing. The film terrified the audiences to the point that many people fainted and blacked out. Others had nausea and vomiting. Some people suffered extended periods of trauma. It was also reported that some had suffered heart attacks during the screening. The scary sequences in this movie resulted in the worst nightmares for even the hardiest of horror moviegoers. The omnipotent presence of the devil is felt in every frame.

For more than half a century, *The Exorcist* took the place as the scariest movie in film history.

More than the horror, this movie is about the forbidden journey into the world of the unknown and supernatural realms and variations of human despair.

Strangely though, the film was one of the greatest box-office successes. The Exorcist was nominated for ten Oscars including best picture, best director, best actress, best supporting actress, best supporting actor, best screenplay, and sound.

I went to the first day first show in New York!

10

Tom and Jerry at the Adults Only Store

The first kiss, the first love, the first job, the first car... the list goes on and on and on. *The first* anything is an experience of a lifetime. Add to it, the first trip out of India. Everyone says they want to maintain that feeling of awe and wonder for the rest of their lives, and not become jaded with experience. So it was with Asli mama and Darius, during their first trip abroad to Canada. Asli Mama was my favourite and 'confirmed bachelor' uncle. Darius was his best friend and my favourite cousin. Having spent most of their life in Bombay, they decided to take a vacation out of India.

My other uncle and aunt, Neville uncle and Parisa maasi had immigrated to Toronto in Canada a long time ago. Parisa maasi was Asli mama's sister. She was also Darius's aunt. Neville and Parisa invited their long-lost family members, Asli and Darius, to their home in Toronto, and they were thrilled and overjoyed when their invitation was accepted.

The first timers took off from Santacruz airport on an Air India flight via London to Toronto, with a three-hour stopover in London. Neville and Parisa were waiting anxiously at Pearson International Airport with two huge garlands to welcome their beloved visitors. There was joy, elation, exuberance, and total delight on everyone's faces. After the initial hugs, tight embraces, and more bear hugs, they pushed their trolley with three bags between them out of the departure gate and waited for Neville to fetch the car.

Asli turned round and round, admiring the new world around him. All he could utter was, "Wah Wah, Wah Wah, Wah Wah!" Darius realized he was now on the other side of the Atlantic, so he decided to think and speak in English. He went, "Wow, wow, wow, wow! Wah, soo waat che! Everything is so, SOOO beautiful and incredible!"

Neville's Lincoln limousine arrived for pick up. Asli was impressed and speechless. He whispered, "O Khudaa!" Darius echoed in English, "Oh My God!" They kept repeating it over and over during the drive from the airport to the city. It was a fairy tale world for them -turning 'first-timers' from the Far East into rubbernecks.

Since it was breakfast time, Neville and Parisa decided to take them to McDonald's. McDonald's had not yet arrived in India. After they were inside the restaurant, Darius leaned over to check with Neville if their three bags were safe in the 'dicky' and learned that dicky made people chuckle because it meant something else – a part of the male anatomy! It was called the trunk or boot of a car. Whatever it was called did not bother Darius. He just wanted to make sure that his luggage was safe.

Asli mama did not know what to order for breakfast. It was not because he did not recognize the dishes; he was tongue tied at the first glimpse of the ebony coloured, silk skinned waitress. This continued for the rest of his trip: Asli mama froze in the presence of all the beauties he saw. He claimed he fell in love with them instantly. But that is a story for another time.

Everybody relished and savoured the breakfast of three fried eggs sunny side up, bacon, ham, hash-browns, toast, and coffee. Asli and Darius were in a food induced stupor and they had not even reached home. But the stupor flew out the window when they entered Neville and Parisa's house. Parisa maasi's home was warm, welcoming, and very tastefully done, but the words that brought the visitors to tears were: *Welcome home, dearest Asli and dearest Darius.* These words were hung from banners all over the front foyer. It was like entering a bower of flowers.

Chilled beer dried the tears in Asli and Darius's eyes, and an hour later, the new guests were stretched out comfortably on soft, leather couches in the living-room. An occasional wheeze, an intermittent snort and a snore accompanied with heavy breathing was the background music of the day. Parisa decided to let them sleep off the excitement of the journey and family reunion. She switched off the television and drew the curtains over day one of Asli and Darius's adventure in Toronto.

The next day dawned beautiful, cloudless, sunny, and bright. Neville had a brilliant idea for his guests. "Let's go to Young Street," he announced. "It is the longest street in the world."

"Will we get young if we go there?" Asli mama asked.

"Or just tired after walking on the longest street?" Darius asked.

The visitors were back in form!

Neville told them it was one of the most lively, entertaining, and fascinating streets in the world of adult entertainment: a tourist hotspot exhibiting and parading an array of live adult shows, striptease, adult movies, and live peep shows. And of course, there were sex toys and adult magazines on sale. "You may come back feeling either very young or very old," he joked.

It was decided that the visitors would be dropped off and picked-up at a well-known junction. Neville and Parisa would run some errands and come back in an hour.

"One hour? Is that enough time to see everything on the longest street?" Asli mama asked.

Neville burst into laughter. "There is no need to hurry. We will wait till you come back to the pickup point," he said, and winked.

Darius tried to look worldly wise and replied nonchalantly, "Okay, let's go."

Asli and Darius were in for a massive cultural shock, but they had no idea! As Neville drove around on Young Street, the two pairs of eyes in the back seat were wide open in total wonder and amazement. Slowly, the looks changed to one of consternation, and indecisiveness. Should they get out of the car? Should they do the drive around and leave with Neville?

Seeing their hesitation, Neville told them he would drive around and return to the meetup spot in an hour. If he didn't see them, he would drive around for half-hour and come back. Those were the days when mobile phones had not even been dreamed of, so all timings and locations had to be decided ahead of time and all watches synchronized. Asli and Darius set their watches to Toronto time solemnly, as if they were going on a reconnaissance mission. Neville stopped at a junction outside a store that sold and displayed adult magazines and stuff, touted live peep shows, and XXXX adult movies. He pointed to a small cafe around the corner where they could wait, in case they missed his predetermined drive-up time.

Still, Asli and Darius remained glued to their seats. Neville threatened to push them out of the car, if they did not get off in the next ten seconds. Reluctantly the visitors got down, like pre-school children who do not want to leave their parents for the first time. Neville and Parisa had the same feeling, as parents did, when they watched them walk through the heavily strapped, thick, rubberized, and very broad, dark, plastic drapes—in order to give the customers exclusive privacy— and the warmth inside.

I am now narrating whatever we heard from Asli and Darius.

As soon as Asli and Darius put one foot into the store, the scene jolted them with five hundred volts of impact. They were absolutely frozen, ice-cold, petrified and panic stricken! The explicit magazine covers, sex toys, life size rubber dolls staring in their faces; loud blaring music, dazzling and twinkling lights, repeated 'peep-show' announcements, coaxing and welcoming invites in seductive voices and live-video screens on view left them feeling like they had entered the land of forbidden fruit! Open-mouthed, aghast, apprehensive, fidgety, edgy, with confusion and turmoil written on their shocked faces, they looked like underage teenagers trying and hoping to slip in under the radar.

But they had been on the African American security guard's watchlist from the instant the first foot had started their 'one step forward, two steps back' entry. He looked puzzled because these guys looked like they were well above the age of consent. Why the hesitation?

To Asli and Darius, he looked like an enraged bull, or a crazed bouncer dressed in his navy-blue uniform covered with shining badges that looked very official. He was very tall, well built, with eyes that seemed, to them, to be menacing and intimidating. He was sitting on a tall chair near the sales counter. His head was shaved bald, and the psychedelic lights overhead bounced off of his head like extraterrestrial signals. When they made eye contact, he gestured at them. Baton in hand, he hollered in a loud, husky voice, "Hey, you guys, what the fuck are you doing?"

Asli and Darius were tongue-tied and absolutely stupefied. Asli, being the senior partner in crime, summoned all his grit and spunk. He tried to look cool, casual, and unafraid, but hoped his beating heart would not jump out of his mouth. Very daringly, he shouted in the direction of the guard, "You, sir, you talking to me?" as if he had his gun drawn for the shootout.

The guard thundered, "Yes, mate, I'm talking to you! Who you think I'm talking to?"

"What's up man?" Asli yelled.

"I've been watching you two. What the hell are you fellas looking for?"

Asli was rattled. He opened his mouth, but it seemed like he had forgotten his words. Darius decided to step up and help Asli. He mustered enough courage and blurted out, "We are looking for Tom and Jerry cartoon videos. Do you have any?"

The security guard scratched his head as though he was thinking how to decimate these two odd customers. He tapped his left palm with his baton, as if ready to thwack them on the head. Tom and Jerry cartoons? Who? What? "Where do you fellas think you are? Blockbuster Videos?" he said and squeezed out and down from his high perch. Before his feet touched the ground, there was no one there. "What the…" he said, and saw Asli and Darius racing back to the entrance.

Asli and Darius ran out of the store without a backward look. In their panic, they ran past the meetup point, realized they had overshot the spot, and stopped to take a breath and wait for their hearts to stop thrashing around. When their legs stopped shaking, they looked at their watches. They had another forty-five minutes left before their rescue mission was due to arrive. They decided not to go back to the pick-up point right away in case the security guard came after them. They walked to the cafe in the next block to wait for Neville and Parisa, taking care to stay out of sight of the entrance to the store.

By the time their pulse rate came down to normal, it was time for them to go to the meetup point. In an aggrieved tone, they narrated the exciting events of the day to Neville and Parisa.

Neville nearly ran the car off the road as he doubled up with laughter. Parisa was wiping tears from her eyes - she was holding her stomach with spasms of laughter. "Asking for Tom and Jerry cartoon videos in an adult entertainment store! Oh my god, I should have come with you guys to see this tamasha," Neville said.

There was silence in the car as Asli and Darius pondered over this.

They had added another *first* to their list – visiting an adult entertainment store!

11

The Gulf Boom

As part of airline staff and more specifically, as cabin crew, we saw a lot of the hopes and aspirations of people migrating out of India. We also saw them on their annual trips back home, eager to visit family, proud to show them what they had achieved and acquired during the time they had been away, and also careful to leave behind their fears and anxieties as immigrants into a foreign country and put on a brave face to the welcoming families.

Air India has always had the honor of carrying these brave souls who leave behind their loved ones to make a living in other countries. In the early days, we saw people migrating to United Kingdom, Australia, and New Zealand. A few years later, it was Canada and America. But it was a whole new world when the Gulf countries struck black gold – oil.

The Sheikhs and Amirs of Saudi Arabia and the Emirates, the sovereign heads of Bahrain and Oman, and the monarchs of Qatar and Kuwait took a leap into another world.

The discovery of billions of tons of black gold transformed the Arab world of camels, nomads, tents, water spots and oases into countries with the tallest skyscrapers, a network of great highways, brimming with shining crushed glass. Gold plated limousines studded with luminous glowing diamonds were a common sight. Seven-star luxury hotels, opulent and classy residential areas and twenty-first century ski resorts sprouted aplenty.

The Emirates became the number one tourist hotspot.

All the major airlines of the world started their main route operations to the Gulf and the Middle East. That was a major boost to the airline industry, and especially a huge gift to Air India.

There was a crying need for skilled and unskilled labour. Countries like India, Pakistan, Sri Lanka, and Bangladesh had abundant supply of both. Hard labour, skilled labour, bricklayers, builders, specialized engineers, scientists, computer engineers, carpenters, electricians, doctors, nurses, and specialized machine operators were the biggest exports from India to the Middle East, and a huge 'brain drain' from India. Millions of labourers and specialists from south India were employed on yearly or two-year contracts to construct, build, and beautify the Gulf countries. This was the first-time labourers found an unending demand for their work, and they migrated in droves to the Middle East, braving inhuman working conditions, and cramped living spaces.

Once a year, or once in two years, the employees would return to India from the Middle East, for a month-long vacation. They would return with their bank accounts heavier with the fruits of their hard-earned labour, and pockets full of new-found savings, and gifts for their families and relatives back home.

Almost all the passengers returning to India carried similar gifts. They all took home the very same, identical items from the same stores, shops, and outlets with the best bargains. It was as though they were all following the same script.

First, they bought an 'Echolac' or 'Samsonite' briefcase or suitcase with a combination lock. Every buyer learned how to set the combination lock with the help of the luggage store salesman. They tried the combination several times until they were sure the combination lock was working. We always wondered if it was mandatory to buy a briefcase before leaving the Middle East, or else they may get into trouble with the customs authorities at the airport in India for not having one!

Another accessory was a small handheld green or brown coloured zipper pouch made of rexine with faux leather strap of the same colour, to hold around the wrist. This pouch held the traveler's passport, return ticket, vaccination booklet for cholera and small-pox shots, one or two packets of 555 cigarettes, one imitation Dunhill lighter, and of course, a wad of Gulf currencies, USDs, and Indian rupees bought at the best possible exchange rates.

With their hard-earned money, they bought at least half a dozen bottles each, of 'Intimate' and 'Charlie' perfumes. They also bought Camay English soaps, two or three packs of six each, distributed in the luggage to hoodwink the customs officials in India. Along with, came a pack of automatic, push-button ladies umbrellas with very flowery designs, and black or silver automatic gents umbrellas.

Every man returning from the Gulf, had a large, but light twenty-one carat gold ring, hollow from the inside, with a red stone set on it. Any red stone would do, but it had to look like a ruby.

A few kilos of dry fruits, almonds, cashews, and walnuts were also very popular. Al Hamra Dry Fruit Dookan was a favourite in Jeddah, with branches in Riyadh, Dubai, and Abu Dhabi. Shopping for dry fruits was a collective activity. Four or five friends went to a friendly dry fruit store together. One guy at a time would buy the various almonds, walnuts, cashews nuts, etc., while the others grabbed palms full of free nuts to taste and sample. Each one bought their requirement in turn, while the others munched away at free samples.

There was constant anxiety about suitcases getting overfull and exceeding weight limits. So, a backpack would be added to the shopping list, since it was prudent to have one more free carry-on hand baggage. To get the maximum packing mileage out of the backpack, it had to contain several partitions with zips and separate pockets - the more the better – including a secret pocket to hide their saved cash earned with the sweat of their brow. Sometimes, the hidden pocket was so well hidden that even the shopkeeper didn't know about it!

With this, everything was packed and ready to board the flight.

One such heavily loaded returnee, with a thick black imitation leather jacket, his imitation Ray Ban sunglasses folded and hanging through one of the buttonholes of his shirt, sweat trickling down his nose, boarded the Air India flight from Jeddah to Trivandrum.

I was the in-flight supervisor on that flight. One of our senior airhostesses, Celia Brown, who was working towards the rear of the economy class was seating passengers one by one. This passenger had both his hands full. He had a new briefcase in one hand, an old green or brown wobbly trolley bag, and a money pouch strapped around the wrist in the other. There was a heavy and over-filled backpack on his back. Another small sling bag lay across his left shoulder and a silver umbrella hung from the back of his collar. I wonder how many things he had crammed into his checked-in suitcase.

The traffic ground staff at the departure gate who checked this passenger's boarding card, could not return it as both hands, shoulders, and back of the passenger were occupied. The passenger opened his mouth wide, and the traffic assistant placed the boarding card, allowing the passenger to grip it between his teeth.

All Air India jumbo jets had a coat compartment with some empty space on the floor at the rear end of the aircraft. This passenger had obviously flown before and knew about this vacant space, to store one or two pieces of his hand luggage there.

As he struggled through the aisle, Celia Brown had to pull the boarding card from his mouth to check his seat number, taking care not to touch his drool. Finally, with his mouth open, he could talk. And talk he did – with a blooper on the way! "Madam, may I put something in your backside?"

Celia Brown's eyes flew open, and she tried to keep a straight face as she saw me behind him, in a paroxysm of laughter.

12

An Encounter with Dara Singh

Who among us does not remember posturing in front of our girl friends or wives? I mean, wife, in the singular, in my case. Never mind that we were not muscular and sinewy, with bulging biceps, like the young men these days, who look like they were discharged from the maternity wards as babies with biceps. But we had one thing going for us – we were daring, bold, adventurous, and stupidly fearless. Add a dose of hot-headed impulsiveness to the mix and you have me – Noshir in the 60s.

To my credit, I did not go out of my way to pick a fight, but I was always ready for one. Perhaps I wanted to impress my girlfriend, and then later my wife, Maloo, to prove that I was her knight in shining armour. Not a well filled out bulging armour, but nonetheless, an armour.

One evening, my wife and I were driving to town from Kalina via the Santacruz subway. Those days, the subway was partly *one way*, the right of way being controlled by two traffic cops at either end of the subway. Between them, they would 'stop and start' the traffic on their side alternately. Later on, traffic lights were installed.

That evening, when I approached the east side of the subway, the traffic cop signaled me to carry on. I was more than halfway through the tunnel when suddenly, another car came from the other side. I was confident that I had the right of way, and the idiot driver of the other car was at fault.

I was more than halfway through. If anybody had to reverse their car, it had to be the other guy. I hoped he would realize his mistake and reverse. But he didn't. I flashed my headlights and laid on the horn. But the car wouldn't budge. I rolled down my window and waved my hand signaling to the other guy to reverse, but... nada.. the car did not move an inch. My hot headedness climbed on to my steering wheel, and my impulsiveness pushed me out of the car. I removed my sunglasses and flung them on the dashboard. I didn't want my *Joe Cool* sunglasses to break. I opened my door, rolled up my sleeves, and stepped out of the car like a film hero. Who did that guy think he was dealing with? I strode purposefully towards the other driver's window. And I gulped.

Half the window frame was covered – by the arm and forearm of the driver. He was wearing a short-sleeved shirt. What was that massive hunk? An arm? A leg? The circumference of my two thighs put together would have been less than his biceps, and, my two calves together were less than his forearm. I slowed my pace. What had I said - *Who did that guy think he was dealing with?* Oh, that guy knew exactly who he was dealing with! A wimpy Parsi named Noshir who had never heard the word *fearless*! Fearless? What was that?

Instantly, I became a Gandhian. An ardent follower of Gandhiji's *Ahimsa* policy – do no harm to others and practice non-violence. This great man had used the non-violent movement for India to gain independence from the British. Who was I to stray away from his teachings?

I looked at the driver, ready to eat humble pie (though Gandhi was a vegetarian!) The driver smiled at me. It was Dara Singh! He was Dara Singh! The Dara Singh!! From the late 1940s to the early 1980s, Dara Singh Randhawa the Great was an Indian professional wrestler, actor, and politician. He had won several WWE world championships. He was truly a world champion! He was given the title of Rustom-e-Hind in the year 1954.

I would like to say I channeled my inner Gandhi and showed Dara Singh the error of his ways and requested him to reverse his car. Instead, I could barely recognize the squeak that emerged from my strangulated vocal cords. "Oh hello, hi, Mr. Dara Singh, so nice to meet you. So sorry to make you wait. I'll just reverse my car out of the tunnel."

I raced back to my car and reversed out in a jiffy. "What? What happened?" Maloo asked. A minute later, Dara Singh's car slid of the tunnel and halted next to ours. He thanked me, flashed a smile at Maloo and drove away.

Somewhere up there, Gandhiji was smiling. At least he wasn't sniggering like Maloo who was trying to hide her glee at her *fearless* husband.

13

No Powerrrrr!

In my career, it has always been interesting when a younger colleague does a first trip to any country. The suggestions, the warnings, the enquiries after the trip – it makes seasoned staff like me feel like a surrogate parent. But I never thought I would literally lead a very sweet, amiable, clean-shaven, pink, and very innocent assistant flight purser to some *hanky-panky*.

Minoo Bhadda was the assistant flight purser with me on a flight to Bangkok. During a lull in his duties, he confided to me that this was his first flight to Bangkok. "Aha," I said. "Ready for some hanky panky?"

He blushed and I felt bad for teasing him. Poor fellow, he was probably still a virgin. But he surprised me by nodding and saying that he wanted to experience the world famous and renowned Thai massage parlours. "No hanky panky," he said. "Just want to go once in my life."

When we landed in Bangkok, I asked him casually that now he was already in Bangkok, what was stopping him from visiting a massage parlour? He blushed again like a new bride and admitted that he was very nervous, very apprehensive, and shaky about going alone. "I will go, if you come with me for support," he said.

I had pulled his leg long enough and thought I should leave him alone. "Any male crew on the flight will happily give you company,"

I said. But he said he would go only with me. Otherwise, he would stay in his room.

The next evening, fortified with a couple of stiff drinks, we called the hotel taxi—we thought a hotel taxi would be a safer bet—and directed the driver to take us to a good massage parlour nearby. As if we could make out the difference between good and bad massage parlours!

The place he took us to had two huge sections. The outer section was like a hotel lobby with a beer and coffee bar. There were about fifty tourists and locals hanging around - sipping beer, whiskey, or coffee. No one gave us even a fleeting glance. Scantily clad beautiful women sauntered in the other section - professional masseuses with big, bold numbers on their miniscule white tops.

By then, Minoo Bhadda's face looked as white as those tops. He looked as if he had died and gone to heaven. The place was noisy. If not, I was sure I could have counted every heartbeat of his panicked heart just by the *thump thump thump*. I held on to him by his elbow, in case he turned tail and ran out like he was in a sprinting race and his life depended on winning. "If you want to leave, I'm sure we can get a taxi or tuk-tuk and scuttle back to the hotel," I said. But the poor guy was so rattled, that he looked at me as if I was talking Greek. I didn't want to laugh. Not knowing what to do, I guided him towards the coffee bar. "Let's have a cup of coffee, and then we will see," I said, as if we were in a doctor's office and he was a child scared of the needle and needed a lollipop.

But who would have thought! One cup of coffee worked like an aphrodisiac on him and confidence came flooding back to his countenance. Gone was the confusion and bewilderment. Minoo Bhadda leaned back and took a few minutes to survey the window dressing – all the beautiful, sexy women showcased on steps at different levels, giving him inviting looks. Then he sat up, pulled up his courage by its bootstraps, cleared his throat, and called out a number. Immediately a lady escort sashayed up to him, as if he had sent out a mating call. Suddenly I felt like a concerned parent sending their child to school for the first time. I even went so far as to tell the lady escort to take care of my schoolboy friend and bring him back safely, before she whisked him away in her arms.

I ordered another coffee and pondered in contemplative wonder at what had just happened. About twenty minutes later, Minoo came back with the lady escort in his arms. He released her when they came up to the table where I waited. She leaned close to me and said in her accented English, "Your flenn welley handsome, but NO Powerrrrr." I nearly fell out of my chair. NO Powerrrrr!!

Minoo looked very pale and breathless, as if he had just won a hard-earned marathon. I almost expected him to say, "Thank God, it's over!" We paid for the coffee and left promptly. He looked very, very relieved to be out of the massage parlour. "*Ho gaya khush*?" I asked him. "You are done, happy?" He gave me a weak grin and nodded. "Let's go!" he said. We hailed a tuk-tuk (Bangkok's 3-wheeler-rickshaw) and I laughed all the way to the hotel. Each time I got my mirth under control, I took one look at his face and began laughing again. If he was annoyed and angry with me, he did not show it.

I am sorry to admit that the next morning when another friend, a crew member, inquired about me missing the previous evening, I blurted out the "No Powerrrrr" story to him. That friend must have told another friend... and you know where this is leading. Much to my regret, the slogan, "Your flenn welley handsome, but NO Powerrrrr!!" spread like wildfire and became the story of the year in Air India. But Minoo Bhada was such a great sport that he would laugh louder than the rest. I truly believe he enjoyed the story more than others did and was proud of the urban legend he created.

In later years in Air India, if and when some woman hit on me, and received no encouragement, rebuttal or response from me, they would ask playfully, "No Powerrrrr????"

14

An Ode to my Friend, Vivek Ajinkya

As airline crew members, we always hope to be on ground, preferably at home, on New Year's eve and day to usher in the new year with our family and friends. But one can only hope.

I was rostered to do standby duty on 1st January 1978 for Flight AI 885 to Dubai that had a scheduled departure time of 7:15 am. My family had big plans for new year's eve – attending a dinner and dance party. On 31st morning, I decided not to leave things to chance and to try and make an attempt to get my name off the standby roster. I rode my Jawa motorcycle to the Air India cabin crew scheduling office at the old airport, Santacruz East.

I met my friends at the scheduling section and tried to convince them to release me from the standby roster. I told them if I was called for duty that early in the morning, it would ruin my year end plans. "And where is my invitation?" they joked. But I did not know that I was not on standby anymore. I had already been pulled out and assigned on duty to Flight AI 885 to Dubai, leaving at 7:15 am on January 1st. The same time that I was driving to the scheduling office, the DR (Despatch Rider messenger) message was on its way to my home. Duty calls. I accepted it with a disappointed smile, wished everyone in the office a very happy new year and walked to the parking area. "Don't worry, we will attend the party on your behalf," a couple of them shouted to my departing back, with a guffaw.

As I walked towards my motorbike, my friend and colleague, Vivek Ajinkya, pulled alongside my spot and parked his motorbike. I didn't recognize him at first – he was sporting a long beard. "What's with the beard?" I asked him.

"No money to buy blades," he grinned. "I'm broke." He told me he had fractured his left arm and had been two months 'off' flights. He was certified to be medically fit and was resuming duty.

I wished him a very happy new year and started my motor bike. Just then a thought occurred to me. "Hey, Vivek, want to do a QTA?" A QTA, in airline speak, is a quick turnaround flight – out one day and back on the return flight. Vivek was thrilled. He was bored of two months on the ground. He nodded enthusiastically and gave me an enthusiastic thumbs up.

A few minutes later, we were both in the scheduling office. Vivek Ajinkya was eager to take my place. The schedulers had no problem in making the roster change. I was given one day's casual leave and Vivek was put on my original flight AI 885. I wished him a very happy new year again and left the office.

I had another task to complete. I had to go to the new International Airport Terminal to deposit the bar collections of various foreign currencies of my previous flight at Pheroze Framroze and Co., the foreign exchange bank at the airport. On the perimeter road around the old and new airports, my bike skidded, and I fell on my left side on the road. I knew I had hurt and bruised my left shoulder. But I thought nothing of it. I picked up my bike and finished the task at Pheroze Framroze and Co.

At home, there was great jubilation that I was off the roster. My shoulder was sore and ached a bit, but that was not going to stop me from partying that night. We had planned a great New Year's Eve dance party with many family members and numerous friends at Navy Nagar, Colaba. Great food, great music, and great company!

For a while at the party, I thought my dancing days were over. I could not swing my body around because of the throbbing pain in my left shoulder. Sensing my discomfort, my family made their excuses, and we left the party early.

On New Year's Day, I woke up with more soreness. I could not move my left arm and there was swelling between my shoulder and chest. Even though no one wants to start a new year with a visit to the doctor, I had no option but to head to the doctor.

An X-ray showed that I had a minor fracture in my left collar bone. My arm was put in a sling to rest my shoulder. I was given some painkillers and asked to rest for a few weeks. Vivek, who had taken my QTA duty, stayed on medical leave for two months after he fractured his left arm. Now, it I was my turn to stay at home for a few weeks.

But the day was not done. There was earth shattering news lurking on the horizon.

Instead of leaving at 7:15 am Flight AI 885 had been delayed by thirteen hours because of an engineering snag. It finally left for Dubai at 8:00 pm Minutes after departure, it crashed into the Arabian Sea, barely three kilometres off the coast. A Boeing 747 named Emperor Ashoka. There were no survivors. Stark. Horrifying. Terrifying. Tragic news.

Vivek Ajinkya was on that flight. Less than thirty-six hours ago, we had both walked together into the Air India cabin crew scheduling office. I could not hold back my tears.

If only we had missed meeting in the parking lot by five or ten minutes.

If only I had not thrown that request quite as an afterthought.

If only he had laughed and refused my QTA offer, saying he too wanted to celebrate New Year's Eve in Bombay.

He transferred his left fractured arm to my left collar bone.

In return, he gave me his life.

"I am sorry, my dear Vivek," I whispered. "I am very, very sorry."

Maloo had signed the DR message that came home on 31st December. She knew I was rostered to be on the flight. I was thirty-six years old. But for a strange unexplainable quirk of fate, she could have been a widow trying to raise a seven- and eleven-year-old by herself. Common sense told her that I would not have reported for the flight because of my fracture. I would have reported sick on the phone and sent in medical reports later. But common sense had no place in her sorrow and grief. Destiny had made the motorbike skid that day.

Friends and family streamed in and out of the house all day every day to support and console us. But for the first time in our lives, we did not want to see anyone. I was consumed with guilt and Maloo with fear.

In the days that followed, I struggled with questions that had no answers. Every day I whispered these questions to Vivek – when he could no longer give me an answer:

Why didn't I leave the scheduling office five or ten minutes before you arrived?

Why did I ask you about the QTA?

Did you know you gave me my life, my friend?

Thank you, my friend. For your gift of my life.

When the heavy, dark, and dense clouds in my mind cleared a little, I paid a condolence visit to Vivek's parents in Bandra. With my voice choked with self-recrimination and guilt, I started to tell them that their son's death was my fault, but they silenced me with their magnanimity. They already knew about Vivek's flight change with me. They wanted to know about my conversation with Vivek and I repeated everything word for word. They smiled when I told them the joke about the beard. When I told them about the afterthought about the QTA, almost flinging the question over my shoulder as I started my motorbike, they nodded and said it was fate. There was no way to avoid what fate had in store for us, they said.

I left their house more cleansed than I had felt in days. Vivek's parents taught me a lesson in acceptance that day. I have never forgotten it.

15

My Pledge to the Almighty

Let's get serious for a bit about *habit*.

How many of us have grown up with the macho Marlboro Man? We longed to emulate the masculine advertising image of the Marlboro Man.

I started smoking because I wanted to look cool and sound cool. 'Taking a drag' was oh-so-cool back at age eighteen in college. The drag dragged on and soon it became an unbreakable habit.

In college, I graduated from Charminar to the filtered brand Four Square. Started with three cigarettes a day, one each after breakfast, lunch, and dinner. Soon, those three cigarettes a day turned to one pack of ten cigarettes daily. Like every other smoker, I boasted that I could give up smoking anytime I chose. Famous last words!

Someone once told me the meaning of the word *habit*. Take away the *H* from *habit* and *abit* remains – *a bit*. Take away the *A* and *bit* remains. Take away the *B* and *it* still remains. *It* is a habit that is hard to kick. I had become a chain smoker. I would smoke when I was happy. I would smoke when I was not. I would smoke more when I was under stress. Smoking became a part of my everyday life. Cigarettes were an extension of my index and middle finger.

My career did not help any - with its motto of *breakfast in Bombay, lunch in London and dinner in New York.* By the time I became an in-flight supervisor and manager, I was smoking my all-time favourite brand, Dunhill and - hold your breath to get away from my smoke - two to three packs of twenties a day. I was like the Old Faithful in Yellowstone National Park. Instead of erupting with regularity, smoke curled out of my nostrils every 30 to 40 minutes.

My entire world was trying to make me give up smoking. My wife Maloo, and my daughters, Zeena and Jennifer, constantly nagged me. They tormented me to kick the butt, but it was all in vain. How easily we smokers call it *nagging* and *tormenting*. When we are under the addictive influence of nicotine, we don't see the love and care that masks their anxiety.

At times, to please my family, I would crumple and crush almost full packs of cigarettes and throw them out of the window saying, "Okay, I give up!" But like a drunk stumbling towards a drink, I would sneak out of the door early the next morning and pick up those badly crumpled packs, straighten out the firesticks and try to fix them again to have a smoke. If you asked me to give an arm and a leg, I would do so readily, as long as you kept your grasping hands off my cigarettes.

After some time, love and care becomes background noise to the main show. You and your nicotine fix.

My elder brother Rusi, living in New York had a single-point agenda with me. "Hey Noshir, it is enough, more than enough! Get smart and give up smoking!! It will kill you. Why should you be the exception?" was his constant lament. When I was posted in London and my routine was to only operate flights between London and New York, Rusi enrolled me into a full course of six private hypnosis sessions, thirty minutes each. Each session cost my brother US $100 per session.

This New York hypnotist tried to mesmerize me into hating the sight of cigarettes. He assured me and my brother that I would loathe the look, the taste, the smoke, and the smell of cigarettes for the rest of my life after six sessions. He had made us believe that he was a magician who would just say, "Whoosh!" and the urge to smoke cigarettes would disappear from my life. But what I found hilarious and got Rusi mad was that towards the end of my sessions, the hypnotist started bumming my British made Dunhills from me! Physician, heal thyself!

That was $600 down the drain, and I kept thinking, "Boy, I could have bought so many cigarettes with that money."

I continued to smoke in my brother's air-conditioned car. I smoked in their bedroom. I smoked in my bedroom with my daughters in the room. I smoked in the dining room, and everyone complained that the food tasted and smelled like tobacco and nicotine. I had become a nuisance, and an unwelcome guest, but I just could not break the smoking habit.

Until the year 1978.

Maloo's legs, ankles and cheeks were swelling up with water retention. Her creatinine levels were sky high, and her blood pressure hit the roof. After all the tests, my dearest wife was diagnosed with a major kidney problem. The medical name for her condition was Glomerulonephritis Nephritis and she was referred to Jaslok Hospital.

The Dean of Jaslok hospital, Chief Nephrologist and Surgeon, Dr. A. S. Mani was her doctor. And no, I did not make any Noshir-type jokes calling him Dr A. S. Money. The prognosis was a possible kidney replacement. Organ transplants were exceedingly rare at that time, and there was a long queue for kidney transplants.

For the first time in a long while, it felt like the ground beneath my feet was a sinkhole. I was scared, frightened, apprehensive, and very, very nervous. One day, I gave way to my anguish and sobbed loud gulping tears, thinking I was alone. I did not notice that my seven-year-old daughter Jennifer had crept up to me. She settled onto my lap and turned around to hold me by my chin. "Noshir Papa, don't cry. I will give mama my kidneys. No need to wait." She used her baby sized fists to wipe away my tears. That made me feel even more helpless and I sobbed, holding her warm, loving body in my arms.

I was the first person in line to donate my kidney. My wife's aunt, Bahia, was trying to jump the queue, because Maloo was her favourite niece and she insisted that her kidney was earmarked for Maloo, if required. I'm sure there were other people in the queue, but I was too distraught to notice.

Before people in the queue started to arm wrestle each other, Dr. A. S. Mani, decided to do one more biopsy of Maloo's kidney prior to making the final decision on a kidney transplant. He said there was a one-in-ten chance of an oral cure with a medication regimen. The tests from the biopsy would be checked in the hospital laboratory, to see if any combination of drugs could help in curing her diseased kidneys.

When the day for the biopsy rolled around, Maloo checked into Jaslok hospital. My in-laws, Minoo Papa and Shirin Mama, my two friends Ramesh Angle and Freddy Balsara were with me - seated outside the operating theatre in Jaslok waiting for the verdict.

> *Noshir moved away from the worried family members and friends. His constant companion - a red-tipped cigarette - consoled him while tears snaked their way down his gaunt cheeks. He rested his elbows on his knees and dropped his head on his palms – the lit cigarette making it look as if his brain was spewing smoke. It was time for a deal. A deal with the Almighty. What could he use to barter? He had nothing – a loving family did not have any street value. Its emotional quotient was priceless, but its exchange value was zilch.*
>
> *If Dr Mani were to come out from the operating theatre and put his hands on Noshir's shoulder and say, "Noshir, stop crying. I have good news for you. Your wife will not need a transplant. We can handle this with medications," what would Noshir do? What sacrifice would he make in exchange for that piece of news? That release from agony. That desperate hope of an intact family.*

The cigarette forgotten in his moment of angst burned down to the filter, and the untapped ash quivered as if it did not want to drop unless and until a decision had been made. A deal made; a sacrifice promised.

The ash, giving up its fight with gravity, dropped to the floor. Noshir flung the cigarette butt into the ashtray – his mind made up. He would give up smoking then and there. Forever. Was it too late for this sacrifice? Was the Almighty listening?

There was a tap on my shoulder. I jerked up from my reverie – where had my mind wandered - and brought myself back to the present: outside the operating theatre in Jaslok Hospital. I looked at Dr. A. S. Mani with pleading eyes. "Come to my office," he said. "I have good news." I felt as if a 1000-volt electric shock had shot through my body. I felt the shock physically!

I dropped my cigarette and crushed it under my ankle high boots. My sacrifice had begun.

I followed Dr. A. S. Mani to his office; and the rest, as they say, is history.

That was the last cigarette of my life. The miracle was not that I stopped smoking. The miracle was that, after that moment, I never ever craved a smoke. People warned me about withdrawal symptoms, and always sniffed discreetly around me, trying to catch me cheating. They looked at me with disbelief, that giving up my chain-smoking habit was that easy and effortless. Sometimes I couldn't believe it myself. My words to people trying to give up addictive habits would be: You do not need strong will power to give up the habit. You only need strong motivation. Pick your motivation. In my case, it was my wife's kidney transplant.

By the grace of God, my dearest wife is absolutely free of any kidney complications till date. God has blessed my family and it is my deepest wish that he continues to bless us today, tomorrow, and always! Amen!

16

Madhivala – the Marvel, the Healer, and the Magician

How many of us have seen hunched men or women walk with a thick cushioned collar around their necks? Or a cushioned belt around their waist or hips to hold their backs straight? They look like they have aged before their time. We trot past them breezily as if to show that our necks and hips move easily on their own accord.

Until... until...

I started to suffer from a severe stiff neck in my early 40s. The unbearable, excruciating pains were relentless, and I was forced to report sick for all flight duties.

Off it was - to see Dr. S. K. Puri, Deputy director of the Air India medical department. I was prescribed some heavy pain killers and had to get many scans and X-rays done. The verdict was advanced Spondylitis. Many of the cartilages of the spinal column in my neck region had worn down, leaving very little space between my vertebrae.

I had to wear, yes, sadly, a thick cushioned collar around my neck 24/7. Now I was the hunched old man who had to turn his entire body if you called out my name, and not merely turn my head. I was scheduled for many regular sessions with the physiotherapist at Nanavati hospital, during which the vertebrae in my neck were stretched and pulled away from my shoulders several times in each session. I also had to go for specialized hot wax treatment to relieve the pains. In addition, I was given some homework - many stretching exercises to do at home.

I was on sick leave for over two months, religiously following this regimen, before I took another round of X-rays. The result was nada – no improvement even after two months of continued and multiple treatments. I was so discouraged by the futility of my condition that I almost bent over double with frustration.

It was during this moment of futility that my dear friend and colleague, Ronny Siganporia met me. He suggested that I see his brother's doctor, Dr. Madhivala as soon as possible. Dr. Madhivala was a very well-known and sought-after chiropractor (bone setter) but the problem was that appointments with him were booked several months ahead of time. I got even more discouraged, but Ronny came up with a creative solution.

Ronny's brother had a confirmed appointment to see Dr Madhivala two days later which he was going to cancel because he had to travel out of station. Ronny would talk his way through and get the appointment switched to me.

"You want me to jump the queue?" I asked, wincing when I uttered the word *jump* as if I had to jump physically with my stiff neck.

"No jumping," Ronny said. "My brother or my friend – what difference does it make?"

I had, of course, heard of the many miracle cures of Dr. Madhivala. I also knew about the world famous 'Madhivala oils and ointments.' However, by this time, I was feeling so low about my problems, that I had my own apprehensions and doubts. Ronny convinced me to at least check him out and give it a try, so I went along with the idea. Very reluctantly.

On the appointed day, Ronny came in his car from Andheri to Air India staff colony in Kalina, Santacruz east to pick me up. Since we were going into town, my wife and daughters tagged along with me for a day out. I followed Ronny in my car. Since I had no appointment with the doctor, I needed to try my luck. For which Ronny had to introduce me first to Dr. Madhivala's secretary, and smooth talk his way in and get the doctor to agree to a switch between Ronny's brother and Ronny's friend.

Success! Soon all of us were taken into a vast room to meet Dr. Madhivala. Ronny and my family were seated in a row of chairs by the wall. I was seated in the middle of the hall. I had taken along all my scans and X-ray reports and my bulky medical file to show the doctor.

To my surprise and disappointment, the doctor showed no interest in my files or my long saga about the neck pain. I already felt that I should not have come.

The doctor asked me to take off my shirt. He touched and prodded gently and felt each vertebrae, behind my neck, and also parts of my spine and shoulders with his fingers. He made me sit down on a chair and went behind the chair. Holding my head, he gave a sudden jerk and twist to my head. There was a loud cracking sound from my neck, and I thought I was done for. I slumped in my seat. The man would break my neck right in front of my wife and daughters. And if I lived, I would break Ronny's neck. But wait a minute... it didn't hurt a bit!

He asked me to sit up straight. One more time he held my head between his palms and gave it another sudden jerk and a twist in the other direction. If I knew what he was going to do to me, I would have never sat in that chair. But my neck suddenly felt quite loose, relaxed and considerably free.

What was happening here?

But we were not done.

Dr. Madhivala made me lie down flat on my back, on a straw mattress, looking at the ceiling. He placed a heavy metal vice, tight between my ears. My head could not move. He asked me to turn 90^0 towards the left, waist down, which I did. Suddenly, he gave me a hard kick behind my hips in the small of my lower back, with his bare feet. If the neck maneuver did not kill me, this would definitely incapacitate me! Astonishingly, I found further relief! He asked me to turn 90^0 the other way and gave me one more hard kick on the other side like it was a kick into the goal post. Goal! No pain, only relief.

With that, Dr Madhivala announced that he was done!

I sat up, but my head felt like it was not there. After months of walking hunched with my head above the neck collar, my head was very loose, and I could rotate my head in all directions. My family was more worried thinking my neck may have been broken, the way it moved. I felt like Megan (Linda Blair) in the movie, 'The Exorcist'.

This was nothing short of a miracle! A miracle right under Ronny and my family's eyes. Not hypnotism. Not mesmerism. Not a gimmick.

I was cured!

I was blessed!

I could not believe what happened next.

Dr. Madhivala refused to accept payment in any form. Neither in cash, nor in kind. Not just me, but from any of his patients. He believed that his healing power was a gift from the Almighty and if he monetized that gift, he would lose his healing powers.

Dr. Madhivala worked for mankind.

When I described this miracle to Dr. S. K. Puri the next day, he was very skeptical and cautioned me that this was only a temporary treatment. He scheduled me for another round of CT scans and X-rays in Nanavati hospital. The reports showed new and major changes in my spine for the better.

This incident is forty years old. I was forty then. I am eighty now. I've lived a Spondylitis-free life since then. Dr Madhivala's miracle has held till date.

Dr. Madhivala is no more. What would I do if I needed his healing hands again? The great healer trained his assistant Dr. Amaria in the art of healing before he passed away.

His legacy lives on.

God Bless Dr. Madhivala and Dr. Amaria!! They are God's Angels on earth.

17

Mother Teresa's Miracle

Every time I mention Bombay, I feel compelled to say *Mumbai to those of you born after 1995*. In the same vein, we have to explain to youngsters that phones were not cameras, and cameras didn't have memory cards, but something called *film rolls*. Film rolls came wrapped and sealed in tiny canisters and we could get either 24 or 36 shots in a roll. But this is not a lesson in the *ancient* art of taking pictures without a phone.

In that era, I owned a Kodak camera. It was an expensive camera, by my standards. In my excitement over the new camera, I used up more than a dozen rolls of film in a few months. I would have gone on to use more, except that the camera got jammed one day when I was clicking a picture. It would not click. The flash did not work. I tried opening the camera in order to extricate the half-exposed reel. The reel was badly jammed and immoveable. Try as I might, I could not pry it out. I did not want to use more force and break the delicate mechanism and render the camera inoperable. The Kodak showroom in town should be able to repair it, I thought. It was not enough to sell expensive cameras; they had to offer repair and maintenance services, I was convinced.

A few days later I took my camera to the Kodak showroom on Pherozeshaw Mehta Road, Fort, Bombay. I requested them to release the reel from the camera. After fumbling with it for some time, and calling other colleagues to try, they told me that they would have to send it to their head office for outstation repairs. I expected the issue to be small and was quite annoyed. What was the point in having such a swanky showroom if they couldn't release a film roll from a camera that their company sold. I took my camera and left the shop.

If you have to run an errand, one of the nice perks of working for an airline is that you can ask to be scheduled to a flight going to the country where you have to run an errand! Get my point?

At the time, I was an in-flight supervisor for Air India. The next day I requested the Air India scheduling section to assign me to a flight to Tokyo via Hong Kong. My plan was to get my camera fixed in Hong Kong - the Chinese being very skillful and nimble in most repairs.

A week later, at Sahar airport in Bombay, before my flight to Hong Kong I declared my camera's name, make and model number on the customs departure declaration form. This was the norm so that I could take it with me to Hong Kong.

I took my camera to a few repair shops in Kowloon. None of the shops could assure me that they could get it fixed in the limited time that I would be in Hong Kong. Let me go back one step – with confusion written on their face, none of the repair guys could figure out what had gone wrong with the camera and why it was so badly jammed. Their unhelpful "Buy new camella! Ha, ha!!" was getting me quite irritated. So much for my assumption that I would find skillful repair stores in Hong Kong. Disappointed and discouraged, I took my camera with me to the next stop – Narita in Tokyo.

I got the same response there. From Kodak shops, no less! What kind of company did not stand by the products they made? "No repair. Much cheaper to buy nu camella!" is all I heard. Frustrated, I gave up on the idea of repairing the camera. My ploy of flying to Hong Kong and Tokyo for a personal errand was a waste. Even though we touched Hong Kong on the return flight three days later, I did not bother trying to get the camera fixed.

My last leg home was from Hong Kong to Calcutta (*Kolkata to those of you born after 2001.*) The airport manager at Hong Kong informed us that we were to fly a VVIP to Calcutta. Still brooding over my non-functioning camera, I nodded moodily and walked on. "Mother Teresa," he said. I stopped in my tracks, all thoughts of the camera dissolving like out-of-focus photos. Mother Teresa. 'The' Mother Teresa. Even to utter her name, one had to take a solemn breath before that. Mother Teresa – the Roman Catholic nun and missionary. Mother Teresa – who founded the Missionaries of Charity. Mother Teresa – Nobel Prize winner. Mother Teresa - declared a saint by the Roman Catholic Church after her demise.

When I informed the crew about our VVIP guest, they were all very excited. Immediately a cry went around asking if anyone had a camera. "Noshir has one," one of them said. "I saw him fill out the customs declaration form in Bombay." There are several times in my life when I have hoped the ground beneath me would open up and swallow me, but that wish was at its peak that day. I told them that my camera was not working and that I had failed in getting it repaired. Their faces fell. We checked with the cockpit crew, and none of them had a working camera on board.

Boarding had started and we were honoured to welcome the diminutive, very sweet, loving, radiant, devout, saintly, and very, very angelic Mother Teresa on board. We were floored to see her in person.

Desperate, my crew cajoled me and tried their best to convince me to check out the camera one more time. Irritated, more at myself than the others, I told one of my crew members to take it out from my briefcase and check it out himself, if he thought I was lying. My purser brought the camera to me. "See," I said, and pressed the jammed button to prove my point. Click! The most beautiful music I had ever heard. I was absolutely shocked, astonished and stunned – lo and behold, my camera clicked! With a blinding flash! I couldn't believe my eyes and my ears. A miracle had come to life right before our very eyes. It truly was like divine intervention. Mother Teresa! It was her!

The camera showed the reel was halfway through and there were about ten shots left in the roll. We were beyond excited – we were giddy with excitement, almost delirious. We took the camera to the upper lounge where Mother Teresa was seated. I spoke to her, stammering, of course, and explained the story of the malfunctioning camera and its resurrection. She just gave me a beatific smile in return and agreed to take pictures with us.

Since we had only nine or ten shots left, we decided to form small groups, so that everyone got a chance to be in this impromptu photo shoot. Nine historical, cherished, glorious pictures. Although the camera clicked and flashed with each shot, I was on tenterhooks in case it got stuck again or even worse, in case the camera was merely clicking and flashing without taking any pictures. I had to wait till I reached a photo studio in Bombay to have the film developed.

After touching ground, I was at the nearest photo studio the first thing the next morning. I was jittery while I waited for the camera to be taken to the dark room and the verdict to be announced. The studio owner came out of the darkroom beaming and confirmed to me that there were nine beautiful group pictures with Mother Teresa in the roll. We were so happy that I slapped him on his back and he congratulated me as if we had birthed nonuplets in the dark room.

I made copies immediately and sent them to all the crew members via the Air India transport department. Those days, there were no mobile phones and very few of us had landlines. But all the crew members managed to reach me and thank me profusely for allowing them to take part in the miracle.

I still have those nine pictures with me and I will treasure them forever.

What happened on that flight between Hong Kong and Calcutta? I can only say that Saint Mother Teresa truly performed a miracle for us, 30,000 feet above ground level. We were all blessed to be a part of this.

18

Missing my VVIP Flight

We live in an era where political heads of state have their own aircraft, and are rarely, if never, seen on commercial flights. If I were working for an airline now, I would never get the chance to be a crew member on a flight that the Prime Minister takes.

Back in 1971, I was scheduled on a VVIP flight with Prime Minister Indira Gandhi on her flight to Moscow. There was always a frisson of excitement when I was assigned to a VVIP flight, but this was exceptionally prestigious. The flight was to depart Bombay at 5:30 am for Delhi and then proceed to Moscow.

I was fully dressed in my uniform for my early morning pickup, when my father complained of a shooting pain in his chest that radiated up his left arm. This was not my father's first heart attack. So, I was familiar with the drill. I placed two sorbitrate SOS pills under his tongue and gave him two aspirins and some water. He felt a bit better and got some relief from the pain. We had bought some time with the emergency medication, but I knew I had to rush my dad to the nearest hospital.

It was 3:15 am in the morning. Fortunately, a taxi had come to the next building to drop someone from the airport. I got my father into the taxi and told the driver to take us to Petit Parsi General Hospital in South Bombay on Warden Road. At that time in the morning, there was no traffic and soon, my father was admitted into the ICU under Dr. F. E. Udvadia.

These were the days before mobile phones. In fact, I did not even own a regular phone – what we call a landline, these days. I used the phone in the hospital to call Air India Crew Movement Control (Air India, Flight Operations office). I explained my emergency and my inability to join my crew members on the VVIP flight.

Much later, I came to know that my wife, Maloo, had already informed the driver had come who had come to pick me up, that I had to rush my father to the hospital and would not be able to make the flight. The driver was very enterprising and took the initiative to do some scheduling on his own. He rang the doorbell of our deputy chief flight purser, Mr. Peter Ryan in the next building in our Air India staff colony and explained the situation to him. Mr. Ryan jumped to my rescue by getting dressed, packed and reported for the flight in my place.

The VVIP flight leaving Bombay was delayed by less than twenty minutes. The Prime Minister, Mrs. Indira Gandhi and her envoy boarded the flight in New Delhi, and everything went according to plan.

I was very grateful to my friend and my boss, Mr. Peter Ryan who saved the day for me.

The next day, I received an urgent message from the Air India Admin Section to see the chief flight purser and explain the reason for missing an all-important VVIP flight. They set up a committee panel for this purpose.

I submitted a copy of my father's ICU admission form to the committee. The time of the hospital admission and scheduled departure of the flight were at the same time. The inquiry panel was concerned and understanding of my father's condition. I was let off with a mild warning for pulling out at the last minute from a VVIP flight.

A few days later my father got discharged from the hospital and we brought him home. The next morning, he was at the Elphinstone Parsi Gymkhana playing rummy with his friends at the club.

Later, I was told by Dr. F. E. Udvadia that I had saved my dad's life by rushing him to the ICU in time. Any further delay would have been fatal. He also told me that in his years of practice as a cardiologist, my father was his only patient, who had survived not less than five major heart attacks.

In my life, my father was my VVIP.

19

Love at First Sight

Everything in my life had to be momentous and larger than life. The same can be said for the date of my retirement. 31st December 1999. The last month of the year, the last day of the year, the last day of the century, the last day of the millennium. When the entire world was waiting with bated breath to see if all computer programs would work for Y2K – the turnover of the century; if life-saving medical equipment would stop working; if airplanes would fall out of the sky; and so on, I picked that day to hang up my Air India uniform cap on a thirty-eight-year career at Air India.

A long innings and the saddest day of my life.

In those thirty-eight years, I had been a flight purser, senior check flight purser, an in-flight supervisor, and promoted to senior manager, in-flight service department. Thanks to Air India, I had several overseas postings and, my family, and I had the good fortune to be exposed to different countries and cultures for long periods of time. At other times, I was at the base station in Bombay and flew out to various international destinations for a week or so. Back in Bombay, I was not on duty until the next flight, and that gave me time with my family.

During my tenure with Air India, and even today, I always say, "If you love what you do, you will not have to work a single day in your life."

I left my dream job with a million memories - mostly good and at times, excellent. If I had to live my life all over again, give me the very same job with the very same colleagues and friends, and of course, the very same airline. My airline has given me so much. Far, far more than any expectations I ever had.

In the same breath I would say: I choose, I elect, and I aspire to have the very same family - my wife Maloo, my two daughters Zeena and Jennifer, and their families.

In the mid-80s, my friends and colleagues often talked about money matters: assets, savings, and finances. Most of those who started their careers the same time as me, and even those who had joined after me owned homes, second homes, investment properties, and built a comfortable nest egg for their retirement years.

On the other hand, I had worked for twenty-five years and did not have anything to show for it by way of assets. We lived in a very nice apartment given by Air India, in the Old AI colony, paying nominal monthly rent. For someone who had fled Shimla as a five-year-old and seen his parents lose everything and build up their lives again, I was happy that we were very comfortably placed, enjoying our lives, loving it every minute of it.

However, the 'very nice apartment given by Air India' and the 'nominal monthly rent' would disappear the day I retired from service. It was time to get serious about getting a roof over our heads. This revelation came to me a little late in the day - in the year 1985, when one of my colleagues was discussing his plans for retirement. I realized I had fifteen years to retirement. Though it looked like a long time, was it enough time to buy a house, get my two daughters married, and amass enough savings to build a nest egg for my wife and me for our sunset years?

Looking back at my years of fun and frolicking, it seemed a steep uphill task; and, all my uphill views were when I prepared the passengers in the airplane for take-off. When I was in one of my rare sombre moods, I mentally compared my savings, resources, and finances with that of my other colleagues and friends. Even though my lack of assets made me feel like a pauper, I told myself, I did not have any regrets. I continued with my philosophy of "Khao, Piyo, Karo Anand, Tel Lagaavey Dev Anand!" (Eat, drink, and make merry. Tomorrow will take care of itself.)

But the seed had been planted and there was a niggling thought at the back of my head. I had only fifteen years left to achieve many crucial, mandatory, and obligatory needs and requirements before I retired, no matter how much I made merry.

With firm resolve, I decided to let the seed sprout and grow and put out tender shoots. I took my first step towards putting a roof over our heads and met a couple of house brokers. I asked them to focus on Kalina, Santacruz east, where we had already lived for the past twenty years.

We saw some two-bedroom apartments - some ready to occupy, and some still under construction. The ones we could afford did not appeal to us; and, the ones we liked, we could barely afford. We spent the next two months in this dissatisfied state, when I called a break to this window shopping. We also had to get ready for my next posting which was in London. I told myself that we would continue looking after three months when we returned from London.

We always travelled together as a family when I went on international postings. Every day was a paid holiday! Zeena and Jennifer, my daughters, studied in Air India Modern School from the Junior KG to SSCE (the final year of school), and their school made it possible for them to be with their parents and get an education without a break. Therefore, going away on foreign postings with my wife and daughters for extended periods became the norm.

The principal of the school, Ms. Rose D'Souza was a darling lady, and a very, very dear friend of ours. My wife, Maloo, taught French part-time at the same school. All the teachers and the administrative staff loved my daughters.

Luckily for us, both my daughters ranked high in their class. So the principal of the school, not only gave them permission to take a break from school for three to five months at a time, but also sent us regular class homework, a detailed progress report of different subjects in the classes, and other school stuff for my daughters. Maloo did the rest. AI cargo and AI mail came in very handy at that time. Sometimes homework would even be hand delivered by the flight purser to wherever I was posted, like high-level diplomatic papers delivered to an embassy!

Back to my house hunting.

A week before our posting to London, one of my regular brokers, Mr. Kotiyan, waved me down from my car on the road next to Kalina market. He wanted to show me one more ready-to-occupy apartment close by, in Sunder Nagar. I was reluctant because we were in the middle of processing tickets for London and New York, visas for London, New York, and Canada, medical overseas insurance, medical formalities, packing and other chores. However, Kotiyan was very insistent. Without any invitation, he opened the passenger side door and sat down, saying, "Chalao. Dekho tau sahi." (Drive, let's go see!) Top floor, two bedrooms, three balconies, he said. Pshaw! I had heard this kind of seduction before.

I gave an exasperated sigh – I had so much to do – and followed his directions with my foot pressed down on the accelerator. I wanted to get it over and done with. We reached in five minutes.

Golden View! I was intrigued.

We went up to the sixth floor. He took the keys from the neighbour and opened the door. We entered. Kotiyan did not say a word but stood back and watched my face with a grin. I was dumb struck.

The two-bedroom apartment was brand new, newly painted, and newly polished. It had three open balconies. Not one, not two, but three! It was beautiful - semi-furnished, almost ready to move in.

I was thrilled! In my excitement I blabbered. "I like the name, Golden View. I like Sunder Nagar, and my best friend, Ramesh Angle lives in the next building," I said, as if all that would suddenly make the apartment affordable for me. "How much?" I asked. Might as well slink out in disappointment instead of building castles in the air.

The neighbour said the owner was expecting seven lakh rupees. Oops! Double Oops! As if to make it worth more, he said the apartment belonged to the renowned Bollywood character-artist and celebrity writer, Mr. Kader Khan. My closest connection with the film world was the great comedian, star actor Mehmood. He used to visit us often in Air India Colony, and would enjoy his time with my daughters and all the children of our building. I was determined to do a little name-dropping, if it got me closer to my dream house.

In 1985, seven lakh rupees was a sizeable amount. It is equivalent of two crores plus, in current day value. I had nowhere close to that amount. But I wanted to buy the apartment and live in it! With my irrational optimism, I told Kotiyan we would drive down to Santacruz West and meet Mr Kader Khan. As we drove through the gates of his lavish and magnificent house, I thought this is the gossamer that pipe dreams are made of.

Mr Kader Khan was a surprise package: he was sweet, charming, very pleasant, and very, very likeable. He cracked open a bottle of beer and we warmed towards each other over a cold beer. Before I got too warm, I dropped Mehmood's name casually into the conversation! I do not know if it was this, or my eagerness and joy to meet him, or my enthusiasm about the apartment, but Mr Khan decided that his apartment had my name written all over it. Or maybe it was because I was a Parsi. Once he knew that, Mr. Khan told me he loved Parsis, and had also done some character roles in movies as a Parsi gentleman. I am vain enough to think that my irresistible personality knocked him over with a feather.

I told Mr. Kader Khan that I had only three lakh rupees available right away. I could take loans against my provident fund and some personal loans and pay him after my return from London three months later, though I would try to pay him earlier than that if I could manage the paperwork from London.

Mr Khan just sat there but did not reply. After a minute or so, he asked me if my family liked his apartment. I told him my family did not know anything about it yet. I had myself found out about it less than two hours back through our broker, Kotiyan. He excused himself, walked inside. I thought I had blown it and kissed goodbye to my dreams. Maybe after a while, the maid or the cook would come out and lead me to the door. To my relief, Mr. Khan came back to the living room with a bunch of keys. He handed over the bunch to me. "The apartment is yours," he said. I was bewildered. I stuttered, I stammered. I did not know what to say.

I placed the bunch of keys gingerly on the centre table. I did not want to let go of it, feeling as if I was giving up on the apartment. I told him I had come directly from Kalina market, after meeting our broker, Kotiyan, on the road. I was not carrying cash or my cheque book.

Mr. Khan took the keys from the centre table and pressed it back into my palm. "Noshir, you are a Parsi Bawaji. Here, please take the keys. Show the flat to your wife and we will talk tomorrow."

Saying that, he opened another bottle of beer and filled my glass. We raised our glasses in toast to each other.

The only other time in my life that I felt a similar sweet and warm electric current going through me was when my wife's nephrologist—after doing a minor surgery and a biopsy on my wife—had come out of the operating theatre to give me the good news that she would not need a kidney transplant after all. Her kidneys would function normally again, with oral medication. Till today my wife's kidneys work perfectly.

Moments like these are to be cherished in the corners of our memory.

I drove out of Mr. Khan's house in a daze. The final sale amount for apartment #14 of Golden View had not yet been finalized. I had no idea how I would corral the amount to close the deal. But I had walked out with the keys to the apartment. The keys to the four built-in cupboards. The keys to the line of kitchen cabinets. And most important – the keys to the main door.

The next morning, I took my wife and daughters to see the apartment. I did not give them a description ahead of time. I pretended that it was just another apartment the broker was pestering me to see. Needless to say, it was love at first sight! For some time, they refused to believe me and thought I was stringing them along. Once they were convinced, they could not contain their excitement.

We went to Mr. Khan's house. This time we met Mrs. Kader Khan. Mr. Khan said he had spoken to Bollywood celebrity, Mehmood, about us. Mehmood said he knew us and was very happy that we were buying the apartment. But this was not the end: Mr. and Mrs. Kader Khan had decided that since I did not have much savings, they would sell the apartment to us for five lakh rupees, two lakhs less than the original price. I paid them three lakhs across the table, and the remaining two lakhs after I returned from the posting.

What started as a pipe dream turned into a reality. Sometimes angels come in different forms. We have to recognize and be ready to embrace them. Ours came as Mr. and Mrs. Kader Khan. God bless our angels!

20

Fate and Destiny!

When a person is gracious, helpful, obliging and thoughtful, he exudes a congeniality that makes him well suited for random acts of kindness. So it was with Freddy Balsara.

I met Freddy Balsara for the first time on a flight where he was my trainee assistant flight purser (AFP). But by the time the flight landed, I felt like I had known him all my life. On that runway, we landed on an exceptionally special and good friendship.

Freddy lived in Dadar, but he was a frequent visitor to our house in Air India colony. The difference in our ages was about fourteen years, so for me it was like the connection my older brother Rusi had with me. Over the years, he became a family fixture.

Freddy was well spoken and had a command over a wide vocabulary. But there was one word he did not know because it was missing from his vocabulary. The word 'No'. He could not say 'No' to anyone who asked him to do something. Word got around, and once people knew you could ask anything of Freddy, he would give it to you or do it for you without a second thought, it led to lot of people taking advantage of him. I would caution him, and even berate him, but all I got in return was a benign smile.

On our second flight together, but Freddy's first trip to Hong Kong, he was carrying no less than a dozen film rolls of twenty-four and thirty-six shots each. I winked at him and asked, "Couldn't get it developed in Bombay? Didn't want anyone to see what photos you took?" even though I knew colour film rolls were expensive to get developed in India. Freddy shook his head dolefully and told me that some staff from crew scheduling and some others from movement control operations section had given them to him to get it developed in Hong Kong. We all did favours for non-flying crew colleagues on our trips abroad, and they always reimbursed us. So, I thought nothing of it.

It was late in the evening when we landed in Hong Kong, but Freddy stepped out immediately to the photo store, near Hotel Miramar in Kowloon where we stayed, to give the film rolls for development. By the time he joined us, we were on our second drink.

The next afternoon, after lunch, all of us headed to the famous Chinese 'Change Alley' for shopping at bargain prices. Between us, we bought an assortment of tee-shirts, jeans, toiletries, and other items for ourselves and family members back in Bombay. Freddy Balsara refrained from shopping, though we urged him to get something for his girlfriend back in Bombay, even if he didn't want anything for himself.

Later in the afternoon we stepped out to the supermarket near the hotel to buy some grocery items that were not easily available in India. Items like cheese, chocolates, Tang, noodles, soup packets, cereals, etc. This was in the early 70s when the Indian market had not 'opened up' as we like to say. Freddy ran across to the photo studio and picked up the developed photos he had given the previous evening, before joining us.

Some of us took shopping carts, while others picked up shopping baskets. But Freddy walked in with his hands in his pockets. I raised my eyebrows at him, and he shrugged. Later, in the hotel room, I told him this was his first trip to Hong Kong, and didn't he want to take something back for his girlfriend? He looked regretful and said that he had used all his layover allowance to get those film rolls developed. "Take the money from me," I said. "Once they reimburse you in Bombay, you can return the money to me." Freddy shook his head and gave me a very comical look. "I don't even know whose films they are, Noshir," he said. "They were all dumped on me." I didn't know whether to sympathise with him or knock some sense into his congenial head.

Early the next morning, I dragged him to the supermarket as soon as it opened. I forced him to take some money from me and buy some token gifts to take back home. After a lot of dilly-dallying, he bought a few bars of chocolate and a gift set of three perfumed soaps for his girlfriend. I only hope he did not give it to anyone else because his 'No' had gone missing!

On another flight, a crew member, airhostess Priya had a damaged suitcase. The hotel porters in London had dropped her suitcase from the baggage trolley. A pile of luggage had toppled down, and the handle and lock of her suitcase were broken beyond repair. Helpless, she tried to drag her suitcase to her room. Freddy Balsara immediately volunteered to lend his own suitcase to her, saying he had carried two medium ones on this trip instead of one large.

Priya asked him over and over again if he was sure he could manage with one medium suitcase. Freddy assured her that he could fit all his stuff in one suitcase. He had packed light, anyway. Freddy emptied one of his bags and took it to Priya's room. He said he would take it back from her in Bombay. Priya thanked him several times for his help.

The next evening, while checking out from the hotel for the return flight to Bombay, Priya noticed that Freddy had one medium suitcase and another large shopping bag filled with some of his shirts, pants, toiletries, and two pairs of shoes. Though the shopping bag could not be locked, it could be closed shut with the zip. She realized that Freddy had given his second bag to her so that she was not inconvenienced, and he carried his clothes, toiletries, etc. in an open zip shopping bag. Not wanting to embarrass him, she pretended that she did not notice it. But word got around among the crew and air hostesses about Freddy's thoughtfulness and generosity.

In 1985, I was posted to London for four months. As was the norm on long stints, I had taken my family with me. My posting ended in June, and I had to head back to Bombay. On all our previous postings abroad, I had always sent my family back to Bombay ahead of my departure, but they were having such a good time in London that, this time, I delayed their departure into June. Yes, in June - when the New York-London-Bombay flights were always chock-a-block (airline speak for full capacity) with holiday travelers. Air India always booked and confirmed seats for the crew member, but not their family. The family travelled on a 'subject to seat availability' basis.

My posting was coming to an end. I was worried and anxious and hoped my wife Maloo, and my daughters, Zeena and Jennifer, would be able to travel with me on my return flight. They pooh-poohed my concern and assured me they could get back to Bombay by themselves. I pointed to their shopping bags strewn about in the living room and bedrooms and said, "By yourselves, with all this? You know the baggage allowance on these flights, don't you?" At which they shoo-ed me out of the room so that they could try on the dresses they bought that afternoon. I fretted about putting them on a flight either before or with me, with all these mounds of baggage.

Somehow my friend, Freddy Balsara, who was visiting his uncle, aunt, and cousins in Toronto got a whiff of my anxiety. He was on a two-week vacation and headed back to Bombay at the end of June. Freddy insisted on taking an earlier flight to London and staying with my family to personally escort them back to Bombay. Maloo was thrilled, the girls were excited, and I was relieved. We would have Freddy with us in London! They made plans for his visit, and what they would do each day, and where they would take him.

On 22nd June 1985, Freddy called me on my home phone in London. He had checked in as the last passenger on Flight AI 182 from Toronto and would be landing in London next morning. We cheered.

He would stay with us and then (in his own words) "escort the VVIP Sanjana family to Bombay."

"Tell Maloo to make three eggs Akoori (Parsi's spiced, scrambled egg dish) for me," he said. Maloo made sure she had all the ingredients for Freddy's dish.

The Sanjana family woke up to the tragic news of a dastardly terrorist attack in the air.

Flight AI 182 enroute from Toronto via Montreal to London blew up and disintegrated mid-air at an altitude of thirty-one thousand feet, killing all three hundred and twenty-nine passengers and crew. The aircraft named 'Kanishka' was blown up by Khalistan terrorists on the 23rd of June 1985, over the coast of Ireland's Cork region. The remnants of the aircraft sank into the North Sea.

Freddy Balsara went down, still with his missing 'No'. Along with another twenty-one crew members who were very close and dear to us.

Maloo and the girls were stunned and devastated. I went into a state of shock and could not console my family because I blamed myself. According to Freddy's original itinerary, he was to have left Toronto on June 25th and taken a direct flight back to Bombay. If only he had done that. If only. If only. Our remaining days in London passed in alternate bouts of crying, silence, staring blankly at each other, at the walls, reading the news, horror, anger, outrage. We devolved into screaming into nothingness as more and more news emerged about the terrorist attack and the crash. Finally, fear overtook my family. I was in the air all the time. That anything could happen at any time to me brought us all closer together and we were able to grieve together for Freddy Balsara – gone from our midst at the age of thirty. Our homecoming to Bombay, which we always looked forward to with great eagerness, was filled with dread and sorrow. We returned to Bombay soon after - solemn, subdued and shaken.

For many years, the Kanishka crash was called the worst aviation terrorism until 9/11 overtook it.

I attended the prayers for his dear departed soul at the Parsi Fire Temple. For years, I grieved for my friend, Freddy Balsara. I had not reached out to him and asked him to come to London. He had called me and volunteered to come. Till date, I know – if I had asked him, he would not have said, 'No.' Did the whiff of my anxiety that made its way from London across the Atlantic to Freddy Balsara in Toronto carry the message of his death? To this day, I have no answers. And I live with the deep sorrow of Freddy's tragic death.

This was the second airplane crash I was indirectly, but emotionally, involved in. Both crashes took place close to where I lived with my family at that time. The first was the crash of AI Flight 885 on 1st January 1978. Air India Flight 885 crashed off the coast of Bandra, a few miles away from where we lived in Santacruz east. Air India Flight 182 blew up over the coast of Ireland's Cork region – we were living in London at that time. There were no survivors in both crashes.

Freddy Balsara was Freddy Mercury's first cousin; Freddy Mercury, the famous rockstar who migrated to England to pursue his singing career and became the lead vocalist of the rock band Queen. Freddy Mercury was born Farrokh Bulsara in Zanzibar to Parsi Zoroastrian parents.

Several times I think of these lyrics from his cousin Freddy Mercury's Bohemian Rhapsody:

> *Didn't mean to make you cry,*
> *If I'm not back again this time tomorrow,*
> *Carry on, carry on as if nothing really*
> *matters*

And I think of my friend, Freddy Balsara, and try to carry on.

21

Drugged and Robbed in Trou aux Biche Hotel, Mauritius

These days one cannot imagine an airline flying to a destination only once a week. Especially a vacation destination. Back in the mid-70s when Air India started its flights to Mauritius, they had a weekly Boeing 707 flight. This meant that if you were a crew member on the outbound flight, your layover was for one week. In no less a place than the blissful Mauritius. Needless to say, there was a great demand to be put on the roster on a Mauritius flight, since it was a great opportunity for the crew to take their families for a week-long paid holiday in Mauritius.

Not to be outdone, my brother-in-law Dara H. Boatwalla and I, both flight pursers, submitted a written request to the Air India scheduling office to request being rostered on one such flight to Mauritius. It was a family trip: my wife Maloo and our two daughters Zeena and Jennifer, and Dara's wife Zarine, who also happened to be Maloo's sister.

All packed, checked in, and ready to go, it was the immigration officer in the departure custom hall who noticed that Zarine carried an expired passport. Dara blamed himself for his oversight and negligence and was kicking himself. Though dejected, Zarine was a good sport and asked him to go ahead without her. It was a sad and dismal parting.

Hotel Trou aux Biche in Mauritius was a vacationer's dream. Our rooms were on the beach. Any closer and the Indian Ocean would have been lapping at our feet. Each unit had two alluring, beautiful rooms with a kitchenette each, and two sit-out porticos with a few comfortable chairs and a small round coffee table. While Maloo and my daughters ooh-ed and aah-ed over the view from the room, I went back to the hotel reception to add their names to the check-in card in the guest list.

"No need, sir," the front desk check-in staff said. "It will only add additional charges to your bill for the room and buffet breakfasts."

I refused his offer to look the other way when three additional members of my family used the facilities for free. I preferred to pay and have everything above board.

Ms. Kuntala Dasgupta, one of the air hostesses, got the room adjoining ours. With a connecting door between our rooms, she said my two little daughters could sleep on the extra double bed in her room. She, very sweetly and obligingly, volunteered to baby sit for us. Our vacation was getting better by the minute!

While we were playing *Happy Families*, poor Dara looked glum and morose, wishing his darling wife, Zarine, was by his side. I asked him to come and sit out on the portico with us. In order to bring more of the outdoors into our room, I tried to open the French windows by the bedside. That was when I noticed that the tall, adjustable glass folding panes and panels between our room and the porch were loose. Some were even missing. Tempted to ignore it - after all, we were in heavenly Mauritius and not in Bombay – better sense prevailed, and I called the reception. I asked them to send a maintenance person to fix the problem.

Very apologetically, the manager came to our room with an explanation. The maintenance staff knew about the problem, but the panels were on order. They were waiting for the panels to be delivered and would fix it with new glass panels as soon as they arrived.

"Can you move us to another room?" I asked.

The manager looked at my daughters running between the two connecting rooms. "I don't have any other adjoining rooms, sir," he said.

I expressed concern that the missing windowpanes were a security risk, and anyone could enter the room.

"Sir, there is no need to worry," he said. "We have security guards 24/7 around all the individual units."

Well, that was it.

The rest of the crew decided to visit the hotel casino late that evening. Kuntala Dasgupta told us she would be happy to stay behind and take care of our two daughters. Willingly, we agreed to the plan. We joined Dara, two other air hostesses, our two captains and our flight engineer for the evening revelries.

Unknown to us, another lady had also joined our group – Lady Luck. For the next two hours, my winnings at the roulette wheel had crossed $500, in Mauritian rupees. Maloo was winning, too. She won a bucketful of Mauritian coins in the one-arm bandit machines. Everyone was cheering us on. We were on a roll! The casino staff complimented us that we had been the life of the casino that evening. But Maloo was worried about our two daughters and wondered if they had gone to bed or were still up. Unfortunately, at the stroke of midnight, we had to head back to our room.

Our daughters were fast asleep and dear Kuntala was awake, reading a book and watching over them like a fairy godmother. We thanked her and went to our room.

I had a chunk of change: foreign currency collections from the Bombay to Mauritius flight against the sale of consumable items, liquor bottles, cigarette cartons, and perfumes in the Air India in-flight store, together with my casino winnings in Mauritian Rupees equivalent to US$ 550. I also had a wallet full of our one week's layover allowance, in Mauritian Rupees. There was no locker in the room. So, I put all the money in a cellophane bag and pushed it into the bedside drawer. We turned in for the night. With a couple of double Bloody Marys in our system, we slept well.

We were startled awake by very loud and forceful banging on the main door of our unit. Groggily, we looked out and the day was already bright and sunny. We had slept in a deep coma-like stupor. I scrambled out of bed, but I wobbled and stumbled to the door. I squinted and found a couple of security guards in uniform with batons in their hands. What had I done? They asked if we were okay. Our heads were spinning. We felt inebriated, intoxicated, dazed, and muddled. Surely a couple of double Bloody Marys could not have done this to us. I shook my head to clear the fog from my brain.

The security guards pointed to the full-length open window by the bed. All the glass panels were out and on the floor. The girls! Were they safe? I managed to shuffle to the next room through the open adjoining door. I found my daughters fast asleep, and Kuntala too was in deep, deep slumber, as if someone had knocked her out of her senses.

We could not wake her up. Kuntala opened her eyes for a few seconds and fell back to sleep. We managed to wake my elder daughter, Zeena. She was nine years old. In her dazed state, she told me that very late at night she heard some men inside the room, talking in a language she did not understand, which we later found out, was French. But she thought she was dreaming since she was unable to move or open her eyes.

There was a lingering aroma of something sweet, something different in the air in both the rooms. I pushed both the main doors ajar to get some fresh air in. By then, it was obvious that the intruders had entered our room through the missing windowpanes, drugged us with some sleeping gas that had knocked us all out of our senses. Confident that we would not wake up, they had robbed us. To this day, I thank the lord that none of us woke up. I dread to think that Dara would have had to carry the news of a catastrophic, calamitous, and disastrous story back to Bombay.

The security personnel immediately called the reception on their walkie-talkies. I called Dara and our Captain and raised an alarm. A few minutes later, some security personnel, the hotel reception staff, housekeeping in charge, Dara, and our flight commander, were all crowded around us. I want to mention our flight commander by name, but today I can only remember his cordial face, but not his name. With all the commotion and Maloo shaking them, my other daughter and Kuntala woke up, much to our relief. They were very groggy, unsteady, and giddy.

A few minutes later, the police were at our door.

The police checked the crime scene. The cellophane bag in the drawer with all the cash was gone. My wallet and Maloo's gold chain pendant and earrings were also gone from her bedside table. I told the police that I had been assured by the hotel manager about 24/7 security. After hearing my story of the loose and missing windowpanes and my complaint to the hotel duty manager the previous evening, the police concluded it was an inside job. There were some staff members in the hotel who knew about my earlier complaint. There were other staff members who knew about my winnings at the casino the previous evening.

The police concluded that the intruders had very silently and stealthily removed each glass pane from the damaged window. They entered the room and sprayed some volatile gaseous substance in both the rooms, knocking us all out. After they took everything of value, they must have walked out via the main door.

The case was getting more ominous and sinister by the minute. A few minutes later, the police and the hotel management got further information that an American couple (guests of the same hotel) were found burnt with gasoline and dead at a bus stop, just outside the hotel premises. I shuddered to think that could have been our fate. Both the cases were interlinked. The crime branch team arrived. Forensic experts checked for fingerprints and other clues.

Dara and I were later escorted to the police station to record my statement and prepare an approximate list of missing items, including the cash.

Now we were on holiday, but completely broke. Add to that, there was no return flight for a week. What was a heavenly reprieve became a holiday with no money. Luckily, an Air India accounts officer came over and offered me an advance payment in cash against my layover allowance, which had gone with my wallet. I gratefully accepted it in Mauritian Rupees to be settled later in Bombay, and we continued with our holiday.

On the sixth day of our stay, the hotel manager called and requested me to come to his office behind the reception desk. The hotel accepted responsibility for the failure and lapse in their security system, and also their faulty and delayed action in repairing the windowpanes in the room. They offered to reimburse all my losses. The reimbursement included my bar collection amount as per the details from my copy of the bar form, the full layover allowance in Mauritian rupees, and an equivalent amount of US $550 in Mauritian money of my casino winnings. They had already spoken to the police authorities and Air India operations department. I returned the additional layover payment made to me earlier back to the accounts office in Mauritius.

I decided not to mention my wife's gold chain pendant and earrings. I had already decided to buy a similar set and gift them to her after reaching Bombay. She was not harmed during the break-in and that was more precious to me than her jewellery. The fact that my family and our dear Kuntala were all safe and alive was worth more than all the gold in life.

Thank you, dear God!

22

Ten-foot Pet Python

We have met my favourite cousin, the late Darius, during his jaunt into the adult entertainment store in Toronto. But there are other Darius-isms that have gone into family folklore.

His visits to any of our houses made him the life of the party, and the only way to get him to stay on was to hide his pants or his black zip bag. Or to ask him where he was going.

Hide his pants? Wouldn't he be wearing them? Yes, he would, but he also wore a pair of pajamas under his trousers. Before he settled down for a visit, he pulled the pant legs off one by one, shook out the pants, and hung them on the back of his chair. Undressing done in the living room, under our amused gaze. Once we saw his typical Parsi style striped pajamas, we knew Darius had made himself at home, and we all leaned back and relaxed. A fun visit rolled out before us.

Soon after his return from his Toronto trip, the visit became even more fun. During his shopping spree in Toronto, Darius had bought a new pair of tight denim jeans. He wanted to look like one of those rugged macho men, but he did not realize that denim jeans had to be broken in like a pair of leather boots. Constant wear makes them easier to slip on, but no jeans designer had ever left enough room inside for Parsi style pajamas. In fact, the designer may have never heard of Parsi style pajamas. But Darius had just returned from Toronto and was eager to make the rounds in his new pair of jeans.

The pajamas and jeans refused to mingle, blend, and cooperate. So, the pajamas were not donned for that particular visit.

It was a lazy Sunday afternoon and a few of our regular friends had dropped by. We were all lounging in the living room, chilled beers in our hands. As was his habit, Darius put his black zip bag away and unzipped his jeans. No one paid any attention because this was the usual routine. Darius tugged at his jeans and peeled them off his legs. Boy, were they tight! Relieved to get them off, he flung them on the back of a chair, and sat down. He was following his usual drill and did not notice the gasp that went around the room. The women pretended that the nail polish on their own toes was more interesting and stared intently at the floor. The men could hardly hold their beer mugs, they were so ready to roll on the floor laughing. Darius looked down at his bare legs and joined the laughter. He was such a good sport, that he took his own sweet time to wear his jeans again, keeping us all entertained at his expense.

Darius was also very superstitious, so we quickly figured out another gimmick to keep him from leaving the happy gathering. While taking his leave, he would first wear his trousers, pick up the black zip bag and head to the door. Just when he was about to step out, we would ask, "Hey Darius, where are you going?" That was it! He stopped, turned back in and sat down. He asked for a glass of water and would leave only after a while. The superstition was that if you ask a person at the door when he was leaving, where he was headed to, or where he was going, his task would remain unfinished and his day would be completely wasted. We exploited this superstition to our advantage.

"Hey Darius, where are you going?" always worked like a charm, and we would have our dear Darius with us for just a little while longer.

In my language, I called Darius the biggest 'Topchi, Fekoochand and Fekoodas' person, but in a complimentary way. He knew how to spin a yarn long enough to stretch to the clouds above so that his bluff and fictitious story could use it to climb down to earth. It was a family joke that Darius would not be able to breathe without telling tall tales. He drew his oxygen from his stories.

One day he came rushing in to say that a Boeing 707 came to a heart-stopping halt inches away from his feet. All while he was minding his own business, standing at a roadside stall in Santacruz, opposite Nanavati hospital and enjoying a glass of sugarcane juice. A huge Boeing 707 at the roadside stall! "I was saved only because I jumped into a huge ditch behind the stall," he claimed.

Anyone would think he wouldn't venture into airline stories in the presence of so many people who lived half their lives inside aircrafts!

But that story was marginally true. This airplane had landed erroneously at Juhu airport at 3:30 am that morning. Our Darius was in dreamland – in his bed at home. But he heard the news on 'All India Radio' that morning and claimed the story for himself.

Sometimes his stories were as long as the python he claimed to have caught with one hand. He could not use the other hand because he was holding his beer mug with it!

Late one afternoon, some of us nephews, nieces, and other family members had gathered at our very dear Vicajee mama and Goola maami's home in Parsi Colony, Dadar, and were shooting the breeze.

After lunch, Darius began, "You know the other day, in the Taloja Waadi, Hormuzji's bungalow compound, after a few beers, I was taking a stroll in the garden. Suddenly, I saw a huge python—almost ten feet long—around a tree. My first instinct was to catch it. When I went close to grab it by the neck, it turned away, and twisted behind the tree, away from me."

We all sat up. We saw the yarn beginning to spin.

Each time Darius tried to grab its neck, it would dodge and turn away. Darius was determined that he would catch it even if it was the last thing he ever did. "And I did!" he said. "One quick move, and with a flash of my hand, and a twist of my wrist, I grabbed the python by the neck, just under the head. It started twisting and wrapping itself around my arms and even my legs, but I held on tight. Remember now, I had a beer mug in one hand, and the python's neck in the other. If I let go, it would bite me!"

One of my cousins snickered, and said, "Why didn't you dunk the python's head into the beer?"

Darius turned to the challenger and said, solemnly, "I tried, but the head was too big."

We turned away to hide our smiles.

"So, I called Dinamai, Hormuzji's wife, you know, to come with the jeep keys. We got into the jeep. I finished the beer, started the jeep and with Dinamai at the wheel, we drove to a nearby snake charmer Sadhu (Guru) around Taloja, whom I knew very well. He is a known specialist in removing poison from king cobras."

"I thought pythons don't have venom," another cousin said, but we shushed him. We wanted to hear how far Darius would weave the story. We all knew pythons were not venomous, but could squeeze and crush you to death, before gobbling you up.

"While I held on to the python by its neck, the sadhu forced the python's mouth open and pulled out the two sacs together with the two glands containing the poison," Darius said. "Once the poison was out, I took it home and gave it to Amy as her pet. Amy feeds it milk and porridge every day. Now it comes and coils up at Amy's feet every day. Very loving fellow."

Amy was Darius' wife. Anytime we looked skeptical at his stories, he would say, "Amy ne pooch!" (Ask Amy.) Poor devoted Amy. Whether she knew the story or not, she always agreed and became his partner in crime, of sorts, on most occasions.

Vicajee mama, who never ventured out in the afternoon, and was lounging in his pajamas, stood up. "Wait, let me put on my pants. I am coming with you to your house. I want to see your pet python," he told Darius.

This caught Darius off guard. "Array! Vicajee, our poor python got infested by mites and termites on its head. Then a lot of red ants swarmed around the wound on the head, and it got infected. The poor fellow died yesterday," he said, killing the hapless python. "Amy is heartbroken, very sad. We had to bury him in our backyard."

But Vicajee had made up his mind to catch Darius in a lie. He told Darius firmly, "Show me where you have buried him. I want to see your dead pet python."

Darius let his yarn run even further. "Uncle, we cannot dig up the grave. It is too deep," he said.

By now, Vicajee was peeved and exasperated, and there were guffaws from everyone gathered in his living room. He asked in Parsi, "Te su ainay te oobho daatio, dus foot under?" (Have you buried him standing ten feet down, vertically?)

Amidst the roars of laughter, Darius distracted the audience with another tall story, and Vicajee mama decided to let Darius off the hook.

But what of the third way in which one could prevent Darius from leaving? Hiding his black zip bag. What role did that play?

Before removing his pants in any house that he entered, Darius would remove a large heavy parcel wrapped in newspaper and masking tape from his black shoulder zip bag and give it to the host for safe keeping in the cupboard. He always winked and said that the parcel had ten, twenty or thirty lakhs cash in it. He would retrieve the bag from the host before he wore his trousers and then take leave.

Darius wanted us to believe that he was dealing in lakhs and lakhs, back in the day when even one lakh was a very big amount. To this day, none of us know what Darius carried in his black zip bag.

Today, when I count the number of my very dear and close friends I have lost in my lifetime, Darius heads the list. One of the many things I loved most about Darius was that he often told me that my daughters, Zeena and Jennifer, were his most favourite nieces. He felt they were the daughters he never had.

This I know was not one of his yarns, but the absolute truth.

23

One Too Many!

The one thing that makes passengers groan over international travel is the unearthly hour that they have to arrive at the airport for check-in. It is the same for the crew members. But the passengers see the crew members walking together towards the departure gate, all spruced up and spiffy in their airline uniforms and are very impressed and satisfied that they are in safe hands. If only! If only!

At all layover stations across Air India's network, crew members check into five-star hotels and supposedly get a good night's rest before the next flight. It was a normal practice for the hotel reception desk or telephone operator to give a courtesy wakeup call to each crew member, an hour prior to the pick-up time. If it were not for that, the passengers would not see our synchronised walk towards the departure gate but would see us sprinting to board before the passengers - ties askew, socked feet, shoes in our hands, and various unmentionables spilling out of our overnight briefcases.

At one of these stopovers, we had all checked into Ashoka Hotel in New Delhi. The wakeup call was for 3:00 am and the pickup was at 4:00 am for the crew of the flight AI 101 from Delhi to London. I was the in-flight supervisor for this flight.

By 3:45 am most of the crew had gathered in the lobby to check out. We were drinking our coffee or tea, and preparing to board the bus for the airport. All except Flight purser Rajoo Mehta. At

3:50 am I asked the person at the reception desk to give him a reminder call and tell him that the crew were waiting for him in the lobby. The receptionist tried a couple of times, but there was no answer. I thought he must be on his way down.

The lift door pinged and I turned to give Rajoo Mehta an earful. Out came Rajoo Mehta in all his glory. He was dressed in the covering that nature gave him. Naked as a newborn! Or to be more precise – buck naked! Not completely, though – he had the Air India uniform cap on his head, his shoes were on his feet, but no socks. He was disheveled, obviously from imbibing one too many into the wee hours of the morning. He wasn't even like Adam, trying to cover himself with a fig leaf. He carried his briefcase in one hand and his room key in the other – which hung from a heavy and bulky brass plate with the room number attached. He stumbled towards the reception desk to surrender his room key. The young ladies on duty delicately averted their eyes.

Now, there was nothing about Rajoo that would make the damsels avert their eyes – when he was fully clothed. He was sweet, pleasantly plump, and an adorable, simple young man. For the young ladies, he was their soft toy, teddy bear with chubby cheeks.

There was complete silence in the lobby and everyone's gaze fastened on him. Soon, there were some muffled gasps and stifled guffaws. Along with three other crew members, I jumped towards him, and we formed a cordon around him. With Rajoo in the centre, we shuffled like penguins towards the lift doors, got him in and into his room in quick time. I had to think fast on my feet to avert an *incident.* I instructed two of the crew members to go down and instruct the crew waiting downstairs to board the bus and leave for the airport. I told one crew member, Abhishek Kapoor, to stay with me. I called the lobby manager and requested him to arrange a taxi in ten minutes to take the rest of us to the airport.

With all this sorted, we got to work on Rajoo. We quickly splashed iced water from the fridge on Rajoo's face. The lobby manager and a lobby assistant raced up to the room to help us get Rajoo moving. They suggested dunking Rajoo's head in ice-cold water. We followed their suggestion. Abhishek Kapoor made some hot black coffee in the room's hotpot and forced Rajoo to drink it.

When he recovered a bit from his stupor, I told Rajoo to report sick and sleep it off. But he fell at my feet, begging me to take him with us on the flight. He did not wish to report sick. He believed that if he did not board the flight, he would probably lose his job. Fortunately, his non-ironed shirt and tie, his uniform jacket and trousers were hanging in the coat compartment of the room. In fifteen minutes, we had shaken him up, dressed him, and brought him down to the lobby again. His bags were already in the lobby, waiting to be identified.

Abhishek Kapoor, Rajoo Mehta and I jumped into the taxi and told the driver to race to the airport. We reached the airport twenty-five minutes late. I spoke to the Commander about the unfortunate incident at Ashoka Hotel. I know both of us wanted to clutch each other and collapse into gales of laughter. The Commander controlled himself and told me very solemnly that I would have to take full responsibility for Rajoo's behaviour if I wanted him to be on board. I was also responsible to see that Rajoo remained fully dressed throughout the flight. He could not afford to put the reputation of Air India at stake by releasing a flasher among his respectable passengers. I bit down hard on my lips to stop the mirth from spilling out.

While this was going on, the assistant flight purser helped Rajoo splash some more iced water on his head and face and made him drink some more black coffee. Rajoo sobered down and boarded the flight. All the crew members were sympathetic and happy to see Rajoo back in his full uniform. Each time they passed him, they gripped him on the shoulder and patted his back before moving on.

A couple of hours into the flight, breakfast service done, cabin lights and window shutters brought down, Rajoo came to meet me in the crew rest area. He apologized and told me he had had one too many the previous night. He thanked me profusely and became teary-eyed. I knew then that our Rajoo was back.

24

Sher Ka Puttar!

There is a certain bravado that comes with the use of some titles or phrases, and we have them in every language. More so, in India, in every regional language. Almost everyone knows the phrases across languages, and no one takes offense to its usage. Particularly Jaggu dada - *Sher ka Puttarr*! Son of a Tiger! It was complimentary, it was macho, and at least it was not Son of a you-know-what – though it nearly came to that one evening.

Jaggu dada was an in-flight supervisor in Air India. That was his nickname – most of us didn't even remember his full name – but he preferred to be addressed as *Sher ka Puttarr*. Of course – his physique justified a title like that. He was tall, strong, and well built, but – come closer, I have to whisper this in case he hears it - also cocky and brash.

It was normal for crew members from different flights to congregate in a hotel room during stopovers and shoot the breeze after the usual shop talk. We met on different flights like passing ships and it was always fun when colleagues you had met on duty on different routes happened to be checked into the same hotel on a layover. Maybe we imbibe more than is called for, but what is a few extra drinks among friends!

Unless that friend happens to be *Sher ka Puttarr*.

We were having a wonderful time in the hotel room. Our Jaggu dada was there, our soft spoken and very amicable flight purser, Rajoo Mehta (now fully clothed) was there, me and another eight or ten cabin crew were there - all together having a great time, and in high spirits, if you get my drift. In very high spirits of the good stuff!

"Jaggu dada, you always say you are a Sher ka Puttarrr," Rajoo Mehta said, holding up his double large drink against the light and squinting at it as if to draw some ancient wisdom. "You always claim that you are the son of a tiger, isn't it?"

Jaggu dada flexed his muscles and expanded his chest. "I don't claim. I am," he said.

Rajoo Mehta pondered this categorical and definitive assertion. Our attention wandered off thinking of other things.

"*Accha*, all right. I want to know - *ke Sher tere ghar aya tha, ki teri maa jungle mein gayee thi.* (Did the tiger come to your house or did your mother go into the jungle?")

There was pin drop silence as our attention jumped back to what Rajoo Mehta had said. He had entered the tiger's den, so to say.

And then, all hell broke loose!! Whisky glasses and beer bottles started flying across the room. Jaggu dada lumbered across the room in his inebriated state and picked up Rajoo Mehta by the collar. Of course, by this time, not only were Rajoo's faculties mushed, but, his body was also as limp as a noodle. Merely Jaggu dada shaking him vigorously would have resulted in murder right before our eyes. I would like to say we jumped up, but the rest of us were also not in a position to jump up. We staggered off the chairs and the beds we were sprawled on and tried our best to restrain Jaggu dada, while all the while Rajoo looked bemused and befuddled wondering what he had said except asking a simple question.

It was a miracle that we managed to drag Rajoo Mehta away from Jaggu dada's rage.

The next day, when we could all see reason again, we cornered Rajoo Mehta and asked him why he had courted death with someone like

Jaggu dada, he still looked confused. "*Arrey, yaar, abhi tak answer nahin mila*," he said. Hey buddy, I still didn't get the answer to my question!

25

JAMBO! Come, Let's Jacuzzi Together!

There is a famous saying: "If you kill one person, you go to prison. If you kill ten, you go to an asylum. If you kill ten thousand, you get invited to a peace conference."

I would like to add to the last one: "If you kill ten thousand, you invite a Parsi gentleman to share a jacuzzi with you."

In the early 80s, I was rostered on flights that had a two-to-three-day short layover in Jeddah and Riyadh. In Jeddah, the cabin crew of Air India stayed at the Marriott Hotel. The hotel had a huge open swimming pool, and I enjoyed swimming in it. This being Jeddah, only males were allowed access to the hotel pool.

During one of my trips, a close friend and colleague, Hashim Arsiwala, and I went down for a swim, and to relax by the pool. Hashim decided to have a sandwich and a cool sorbet by the pool before the swim. I left him there and went to the changing and shower room, past the jacuzzi area.

I had changed into my Speedos and was putting away my clothes and wallet in an open locker, when a very dark-complexioned giant of a man lumbered up to me. It is hard to say that a monstrously huge, colossal giant of a man could have appeared out of nowhere, but I swear I did not see him until he was really close. I felt like a dwarf and took a quick step back so that I could take in his entire height and girth, both vertically and horizontally. Then, I did a double take!

It was Idi Amin. He was Idi Amin! The Idi Amin!! In flesh (a lot of it) and blood.

Idi Amin was the most despicable butcher of Uganda. He tortured and killed over three hundred thousand of his own people. He had the limbs chopped off of one of his wives. He had even admonished Hitler for killing too few Jews! Idi Amin was a complete psychopath. He was obsessed with power. The fusion of psychopathy and power in one man can shake and shatter an entire nation. Idi Amin was the perfect example of this.

I was shocked, stunned, and stupefied beyond my senses. He came closer with his arm stretched out and greeted me in a deep and thick accent. "Jambo!" I knew it meant *Hello* in Swahili African lingo because we had a common inside joke among us in Air India. An aircraft joke. If we were greeted by the hotel staff in Africa with a "Jumbo!" we would reply, "No! 707!" with a grin and watch their puzzled expressions. Air India 747 jets were called jumbos. Instinctively, I blurted out, "No, 707."

Whether Idi Amin was amused or not, he seemed to find it very funny. He roared and shook with laughter. The locker room ricocheted with the sound of his booming laugh. He said, "I am Amin. Idi Amin. I like your fair skin. Come, let's jacuzzi together!"

Let's jacuzzi together? Was that a code word for something? This man was a known cannibal. He killed people and ate them. He was like a hungry wolf, a man-eater tiger that gets the taste of human flesh and keeps coming back for more. He stored the heads of his rivals and adversaries in freezers!

Such a man was asking me to jacuzzi with him? Was he was hitting on me or was he looking at his next meal? His eyes looked red to me. I was standing alone in a sprawling changing room in Saudi Arabia, inches from a man who was a mass killer, an ogre, a cruel, ruthless cannibal, a fiend, and a demon. He was responsible for the death of millions of Ugandans, some British people, and scores of Asians.

My body jumped into panic mode. I could hear my heart thumping. Dumb with fear and loathing, I extended my hand. The size and feel of his palm felt like he was wearing a pair of very coarse and very rough black boxing gloves - rubbery and oily. I managed to slip my hand from his grip and gave a weak, but quivering grin. "Thank you, but I gotta go," I squeaked and sprinted out of the changing room. Was he watching me in my Speedos, licking his lips in regret for a quarry that was fleeing?

When I came out poolside, I tottered to Hashim's table, and collapsed on the chair. He stopped mid-bite and put down his sandwich. "What happened? Are you sick?" he asked. I grabbed his cool sorbet and took a huge gulp, spilling a lot of it on the table. "What? What?" he said. "Do you need a doctor?"

It was a while before I was coherent enough to tell him who I met in the changing room. He didn't believe me. He gestured to one of the waiters, but I didn't wait for him to ask. "What the hell is Idi Amin doing in the hotel swimming pool?" I asked, as if it was the waiter's fault. He told that us that Idi Amin and his family were honoured guests of the Marriott Hotel. Honoured?

In April 1979, Idi Amin and his regime had been finally thrown out of power. He had to flee the Ugandan national capital city of Kampala. The Tanzanian military, and the anti-Amin forces under the Ugandan National Liberation Front (UNLF) took over and formed a new coalition government together with former exiles. Idi Amin escaped to Libya with his families - he had about six wives and forty children! General Gaddafi gave him asylum, but soon kicked him out due to international pressure. Idi Amin and his families were finally given asylum in Jeddah by the royal family of the Saudi monarchy.

I knew that the monarchy of Saudi Arabia had given Idi Amin and his family permanent asylum, but in my wildest nightmares, I never expected to run into him in Marriott, of all places.

Idi Amin did not come out to the pool area for quite some time. I imagined him sitting like a hippopotamus in the jacuzzi. I felt nauseous and sick for all the bloodshed, destruction, and massacre he had committed and decided not to swim that day. But I was clad in my Speedo swimming trunks, and my clothes and wallet were in the locker room. Wild horses couldn't drag me back into the locker room.

Hashim went to the reception and spoke to the lobby manager about the situation. The manager immediately came and met me in the pool area to help. At that moment, Idi Amin came out of the changing room and jumped in the water to join a couple of his sons in the pool. Seizing the opportunity, I made my escape.

Watching him jump into the water reminded me of River Nile. During his reign of terror, there were so many bodies to dispose of, that his men threw them in the river Nile, to be eaten by crocodiles. He had also built an underground prison for his rivals and enemies. Thousands of Ugandans were picked up and captured, tortured, and killed. He also had his own high ranking government ministers killed and beheaded if they upset him.

In 1972, Asian minorities of sixty thousand Ugandans, mostly Gujaratis, were expelled from the country with a ninety-day notice. Idi Amin hated the intelligentsia and the successful Asian Ugandans. He stole their homes, businesses, money, and properties. He got all those classes of people killed. Those who escaped, returned to India using the relief and rescue operations run by Air India. There were daily chartered flights to Entebbe and back.

I was part of the cabin crew as a flight purser and made it my mission to be on those flights. I wanted to be on as many rescue-operation flights as possible and bring back as many families of survivors and refugees as possible to India. I had given my request in writing to the flight rostering and scheduling office.

It was heart-breaking to welcome those fleeing passengers on board. Each passenger leaving Uganda was allowed to take back only US$10 with them. Those who tried to smuggle out more were caught by the airport police and military and taken away. Their money was confiscated, and they were never seen again.

After the encounter in the locker room, what lingered on and stayed in my mind was that an evil monster, a demon, a veritable beast roamed totally free, enjoying his life without a care, without any accountability. He was the honoured guest of the royal family of Saudi Arabia. He was the honoured guest of the Marriott hotel.

Where was the world's justice? Where was the UN? What were the big nations of the world doing while criminals, despots, tyrants, murderers, evil dictators, and oppressors strutted freely in the world without a care?

What is happening to mankind? Are we cowards, or are we all just looking away?

To complete this story, I would like to record that Idi Amin enjoyed the hospitality of the Saudi royal family for two full decades until his death in 2003.

26

Bawa Adam Murghi Chor

If one lived in a Parsi Baug (a Parsi colony) one would have a second name. There was no escaping it. I will explain this strange phenomenon at the end of this chapter, but suffice to say, that sometimes we forgot the birth name of a person.

Second names were used only when one was very young; and, that too, only for boys. The only exception was if a girl was named Frenny and she was pretty. Then she was called Frenny Fatakri which meant Frenny the Bomb. These tags wore off once you had finished school and college and started working. It was unfortunate that the tag of 'Bawa Adam Murghi Chor' stayed with this duplicate Mohammed Rafi all his life. So long, that I've even forgotten his actual name.

There are other Parsi-isms that I will also explain at the end of this chapter.

The duplicate Mohammed Rafi lived on the third floor of the building in front of which my in-laws lived in Cusrow Baug, a beautiful colony. He was known by several names. Some called him Bawa Adam (the first original Parsi), others called him Minoo Mad. But most of the people in Cusrow Baug knew him as Murghi Chor, or chicken thief.

Murghi Chor loved very old, sad, and melancholic Hindi songs sung by the legendary Saigal, the first singing hero in films in the 30s and 40s. "Diya jalao" was his favourite! Every night, he would begin singing into a microphone attached to his night shirt. His *riyaaz* (traditional singing practice) started around ten in the evening and went on till midnight, completely oblivious to his neighbours and their need for sleep.

At 10pm, everyone would sigh and say, "Chalo, chaaloo thaee gayo, ghel-chodio, Mohammed Rafi" (That idiot Mohammed Rafi has started). The more irate ones would shout at him and abuse him, "Aye chutiyaa, bandh kar" (Hey you *!&#!, stop!). Some who had already turned down the bedcovers and crawled into bed, would wedge their heads between their pillows. Others who stayed up late to watch TV would turn up the volume high enough to drown out Mohammed Rafi's voice, but the television programs were equally bad, and listening to them at high volume was a different kind of torture. All these abuses and protests, and the built-up animosity among all the neighbours had no effect on Murghi Chor. He was in love with his own voice! He claimed it was a god given gift and it would be blasphemy not to bless the world with his mellifluous singing.

Murghi Chor had another nightly ritual that was worse than his out-of-tune singing. He cleansed his mouth and throat before and after every singing session. So, the neighbours had to suffer through his 'deep throat gargling.' He swallowed some special liquid and gargled noisily and at length. Many of us hoped he would choke during his gargling ritual.

His companion in the third-floor apartment with him was a pet rooster. Though I don't remember Murghi Chor's name, I do remember the rooster's – he had very lovingly named his rooster Pestonjee.

After midnight, Pestonjee shared the pillow with Murghi Chor. With a rooster, Murghi Chor did not need an alarm clock, and his first 'Kook-Re-Koo' at the crack of dawn was always into his master's ears. His duty done, Pestonjee would make sure the rest of us woke up with his continuous 'Kook-Re-Koo, Kook-Re-Koo, Kook-Re-Koo!'

Having woken up the neighbourhood, it was time to walk the rooster. Either Murghi Chor thought his rooster was a dog, or the rooster had aspirations to be a dog. Pestonjee had a permanent collar: a thick red silk ribbon tied around his worn out, featherless neck, attached to a long nylon rope for a leash. Murghi Chor and Pestonjee were all set for their morning walk as the sun came up. The master walked on the inner side of the road and Pestonjee strutted on a long leash - dead centre of the road.

Cars had to swerve and drive away with a loud honk and curses, keeping a safe distance. Pestonjee in his full glory, bright, vivid, and vibrant would crow at the top of his vocal cords; 'Kook-Re-Koo, Kook-Re-Koo, Kook-Re-Koo!' while the neighbours started their day, cursing.

As the anger and frustration built up, one day Rusi Mistry brought his air gun to the second floor window to shoot Pestonjee. But his wife was an animal lover. "You can't shoot the rooster," she said and stood between the window and the air gun. "Then who can I shoot?" bellowed Rusi, his sleepless nights catching up with his temper. His wife moved away from the window and pointed down the street. "You should shoot that Murghi Chor instead!" Both Rusi and his wife collapsed into laughter. "That is what is called killing two birds with one shot," Rusi said, when he stopped laughing.

But calmer minds prevailed. Violence, vengefulness, and revenge are three words not found in a Parsi Bawa's dictionary.

This story has both a happy ending and a sad one. Happy for Murghi Chor and Pestonjee, and sad for all his Cusrow Baug neighbours!

I would like to end the story here, but I had promised to explain this strange phenomenon of second names among Parsis at the end of this chapter.

Behram was 'Behram Batko', (Parsi slang for Shortie). He may have been a six-footer, but Behram and Butko went well together.

Bomy was always 'Beecharo Bomy', (poor Bomy) or 'Bomy Bakro', (a goat) or 'Bomy Bumlo', (Bombay duck, a fish found only on the coastal shores of Bombay).

Cherag may be smart and very clever, but he would be called 'Cherag Chutio', meaning, an idiot.

Fali would be called 'Fali Fekoo', (bluff master or teller of tall stories).

Faredoon was 'Faredoon Fattkaylo', (Fardoon has lost it!).

Homi would be 'Homi Hando', (Homi the bum), or 'Homi Halkat', (a very mean guy).

Jimmy may have obtained zero degrees in the field of spying and may be deaf, dumb, or blind but he would always be called 'Jimmy Jasoos', meaning Jimmy the Spy. He would also be respectfully addressed as Perry Mason, the famous detective of yesteryears.

If your name was Keki, even if you never ever borrowed a penny, you would still be named either 'Keki Karko', meaning broke, or 'Keki Kanjoos', meaning miser.

Kersi was 'Kersi Karoodas', (swindler). Poor guy! He may have been as innocent as a newborn babe, but he was given the title of swindler whether or he liked it or not!

Luvji became 'Luvji Lapoot', meaning, always entangled in love.

The Noshirs and Narimans of the community were either 'Nolio', meaning mongoose or 'Nautanki', or 'Drameybaaz', meaning drama queen.

Soli was 'Soli Surmai', or Soli Supperchand (Surmai was a kind of fish and Supperchand, a simple apple).

Tehmul would be called 'Tehmul Tooryoo', (a vegetable) or 'Tehmul Topchi', (bluff master) irrespective of whether he ever lied or not.

Lastly, Minoo had to be 'Minoo Mad', or 'Minoo Makori', (a black ant) or even 'Minoo Murghi Chor.' (chicken thief).

Now, it comes back to me. Murghi Chor's first name was Minoo!

Here are other Parsi-isms that I promised to explain at the end of this chapter.

If Murghi Chor's shenanigans had been performed as a play, none of our children would have watched it. Not even if we threatened them with dire consequences.

Every Parsi New Year, it was a mandatory ritual to go to a Parsi Naatak (Parsi play/theatre). We knew it would be filled with 'Koila' (senseless and silly Bawa humour). But we religiously booked tickets weeks in advance for the entire family, in spite of the children protesting, "Dad, don't buy me a ticket. I will not come." The parents would shout back, "It is our new year. We have to go. Period."

The plays were two hours of very typical Parsipannu (typical Parsi style absurd humour): stupid, crazy, loud, and farcical. The same jokes, the same slip-slap comedy about a married Parsi Bawa (man) with roving eyes for pretty Parsi girls half his age. Chaos and pandemonium, confusion and mix-ups reigned supreme when he had some mini affairs on the sly. The man's authoritarian and despotic wife would finally bulldoze him back to his senses.

Happy ending!

The curtains came down, only to open again.

Everybody laughed, clapped, and gave a standing ovation. It didn't matter if the play was good or not. After mixing around during the fifteen-minute break and the interval, snacking on chutney and cheese sandwiches, Punjabi samosas, washed down with cold coffee, we wished each other Navroze Mubarak (Happy New Year).

It was Parsi New Year. Half the Parsi and Irani population of Bombay, in their fancy new year outfits, would be present at the theatre. To see and be seen. Everybody was happy. It all made the play worthwhile.

27

Mother: A Short Story

On my mother's side, I was blessed to have five maternal uncles and three maternal aunts. On my father's side, I had five paternal uncles and one paternal aunt. A total of fourteen uncles and aunts – all of them kind, generous and affectionate with all their nieces and nephews.

My favourite uncle was my own namesake – Noshir uncle, but we called him Nusli.

My dearest Nusli mama (uncle) used to narrate and sing a heart-breaking song in Urdu about a mother and her son. The lyrics and narration of this poignant ballad brought tears to our eyes.

I would like to narrate that ode in my own words, as a tribute to my late uncle, Nusli mama.

Once upon a time there was a pretty, young, destitute woman named Shanta married to Ramu, a young poverty-stricken farmer. Ramu worked the land owned by the villainous village head, Zamindar Jorawar Singh.

Due to lack of rains for two years, the parched terrain was as dry and hard as an endless slab of lava and metal. Even the village well had dried up.

Many villagers, including the village ayurvedic, had packed and loaded their scanty and meagre belongings on their bullock carts. They left their homes and started to plod away, out of the village, looking for some other place with water, wheat, or rice.

Ramu and Shanta led a hand to mouth existence with one meal a day of raw onions, chilies and a bajra roti baked by Shanta on a fire of dry sticks and leaves. Shanta was seven months pregnant. The next monsoon, even if it brought a trickle of rain, was seven months away. Shanta and Ramu were tense, worried, and very distressed. They possessed neither a bullock nor a bullock cart. They were two months away from becoming parents and could not undertake a journey to an unknown land.

Ramu begged Zamindar Jorawar Singh to spare some water from his private well, and a hand full of jowar or wheat. But he was turned away. Ramu, already disturbed and depressed, got a little out of control. His desperate pleading, begging, and crying turned into an altercation with the God of the village, Jorawar Singh, who got his musclemen to beat Ramu up with their sticks and lathis and throw him out in the open empty fields.

When news reached the village, Shanta ran to the open field only to find her one and only support, her child's father, lying dead. Even the bleeding from the head had dried and stopped. Sobbing and weeping hysterically, Shanta ran to the Zamindar - dazed, wobbly and weak with tear-filled eyes - for some kind of help, any help.

Zamindar Jorawar Singh took the pretty Shanta in his arms to console and comfort her. He offered his hand in marriage. Shanta tore herself away, but with a baby in her parched womb, she had nowhere to go. In her agony and grief, she managed to escape from the clutches of Jorawar, but he was content to play the waiting game until the baby arrived.

Two months later, Shanta gave birth to a baby boy, who looked like his late father, Ramu. At the same time, most unexpectedly and out of season, a few dark clouds gathered over the whole village and resulted in very welcome showers. The few emaciated and malnourished families left behind in the village danced and sang in joy, looking skywards to welcome the rains.

The newborn was named 'Paaoosh' (rains).

Shanta was unable to feed her baby because her milk had dried up. She decided once again to seek the help of the village devil, Jorawar Singh.

Jorawar Singh gave her bags full of jowar, flour, wheat, rice, and unlimited access to his private water-filled well. In return, he told her to work as a maid in his lavish home and satisfy his needs. For her child's sake, she broke down and relented.

The mother's milk returned to her breasts. So did the insatiable, demanding Jorawar, night after night. The Malkin, or mistress of the house, was kind to Shanta. She fed the baby mixed grains, some milk, porridge, and some curd too.

Shanta continued to live for her son. She dreamed that her son would grow up and become successful one day and earn enough money to run away from the clutches of the zamindar.

Sure enough, Paaoosh did grow up and became a handsome, strong, and smart young man. He finished his studies from the municipality school in the next village. He was devoted to her and took care of her every need. He also worked for the aging zamindar, became his advisor and one of his personal bodyguards.

Shanta had a million dreams for her son. She dreamt that her son would find a nice wife for himself. Her daughter-in-law would cook, mop, and scrub the little room in her place. She would look after Shanta when she grew old, frail, and feeble. She daydreamed and fantasized that her son Paaoosh and her daughter-in-law would take her to Kashi, Mathura, and Banaras before she met her Maker. For the first time in her life, she was content and happy to be free from the clutches of the old and aged zamindar.

Everything she imagined would have materialised, except that Paaoosh fell passionately in love with a very beautiful lady named Naaz from the nearby city. She was older, much older than him. Paaoosh was desperately in love and became a regular visitor to her dainty yet very small house. He promised her that he would change his religion for her.

The temptress, seductress, and enchantress Naaz accepted his proposal and promised to marry him, but with one precondition. To prove that he truly loved her, he would need to do something for her. He promptly agreed.

Naaz asked him to go home to his mother, slaughter her, tear open her chest, rip out her pumping heart and bring it - live and beating – to her. Paaoosh was stupefied, shocked, and speechless. He loved his mother, but he desired and lusted after Naaz like a crazy wild animal.

In a moment of crazed insanity, Paaoosh, the lustful paramour, ran home to his sleeping mother. He raised a knife in his hand and slashed her throat. He ripped open her chest in a frenzy and tore out her thumping heart.

Gripping his mother's bleeding and still beating heart, he started running back towards Naaz's house. He stumbled and fell, losing his grip. Out flew his mother's beating heart from his closed fist. As he fell, he heard his mother's voice through the beating heart, asking him, **"Betta Paoosh, tuje chotte toh nahi aayee?" My beloved Paaoosh, are you hurt, my son?**

28

Triple Bypass

I am certain that any person who questions a doctor's financial motive in performing an essential surgery, has to make sure he is never under anesthesia when the same doctor is operating on him. Sometimes I like to live dangerously. Sometimes danger skirts my life.

One day, during the first week of March, 1993, *Brown Girl in the ring, Tra la la la la, There's a brown girl in the ring, Tra la la la la la* filled the car as Maloo, my own *sugar in a plum* was singing to Boney M's 70s song. We were driving from the airport to our house in Kalina, and I was tapping the beat on the steering wheel. Life was glorious.

All of a sudden, I felt a sharp jolt of pain in my chest and left arm, and I gasped. The pain travelled to my left shoulder and engulfed the whole left arm. I felt a steamy perspiration on my forehead, and my fingers gripped the wheel instead of the light tapping. Maloo turned to me, my *sugar in a plum* immediately sensed something was wrong.

I was near Vakola pipeline. At the Military Junction, Maloo told me to turn left towards the Air India medical clinic, old airport, instead of taking a right to Kalina. I hesitated for a few seconds, but due to the pain, I turned left. By the time we reached the Air India old airport gate, the pain subsided. I turned the wheel as if to make a U-turn instead of going through the gate, when Maloo guessed what I was doing. "We are already here. Might as well see a doctor," she said.

In the clinic, I walked directly to Dr. Puri's office. There were other patients waiting to see him, but seeing the look on my face, he guided me straight to the couch. Dr. Puri gave me an injection and placed some tablets under my tongue. Before I knew what was happening, I was on my way to Hinduja Hospital in the Air India ambulance with Maloo in tow.

Our old neighbour and friend, Srinivasan Sitapatti, was at the reception in Hinduja. In minutes, he got me admitted to the ICU. Cardiologist Dr. Jamshed Dalal attended to me. In the meanwhile, Srinivasan called my daughters. Soon they were by my side, consulting and talking to all the attending doctors. The doctors decided to do an angiography on me the next day.

I thought all my pain would be gone, but I had the same excruciating pain in the chest and left arm during the angiography procedure the next day. I was sure it was another heart attack. Indeed, it was – a second heart attack. During the angiography they found three major blockages in my main arteries. Two 90% blockages and one 100%. Top surgeon, Dr. Nitu Mandke was called in for a consultation by my daughters and Dr. Jamshed Dalal.

The prognosis was that I required a triple bypass surgery. When I heard that, I wanted to give everyone the slip and run home. I was in good health and only fifty-two years young. I decided I did not need any surgery, definitely not a bypass. It was common knowledge among the uninformed like me that open heart surgery was a moneymaking racket.

But Maloo, my two daughters, Dr. Jamshed Dalal, and Dr Nitu Mandke convinced me that the surgery was absolutely essential and very, very crucial for my continued well-being. What could I do? I convinced myself that Dr. Jamshed Dalal was a Zoroastrian Parsi and would not mislead me. So, the surgery date was fixed for two days later.

The hospital needed a few bottles of blood for my open-heart surgery. A notice was put up at our scheduling office and the airport operations office that, Noshir Sanjana was to go under the knife in Hinduja hospital and would require some voluntary blood donors, irrespective of the blood type. Irrespective of blood type? Were they going to pump in a cocktail of blood types into my veins? No, they were planning to stock their blood bank.

Soon there was a long line of my crew members, some crew scheduling officers, our office peon and even one of our office stenographers, waiting and wanting to donate blood for me. I needed four to five bottles of blood during my procedure, but the hospital pathology and Hinduja blood bank, were more than happy to collect dozens and dozens of bottles of blood from my friends under my name. Finally, my best friend Ramesh Angle realized the situation and stood at the pathology lab and turned away all the would-be donors, with many thanks on behalf of me and my family.

By the time, the surgery date rolled around, my sister Lily flew down in a mad rush from Toronto. My uncles, my aunts, my cousins, my nephews, all my neighbours from Golden View and some ex-neighbours from Air India colony were all there, in support of my wife and my daughters.

A double team of doctors, nurses, anesthesiologists, and surgeons stood by for any adverse, untoward emergencies, since I had a second heart attack during the angiogram. The triple bypass surgery took more than half a day. The next thing I remember is me lying half-awake, very dazed and disoriented in the recovery room. I felt like a science experiment - enveloped in a bubble, full of tubes, a couple of holes in my chest for the pipes, needles, oxygen mask, electronic connections, machines, bandages, and other paraphernalia all around and into me. I also remember asking my surgeon, Dr Mandke, in the recovery room how many more years I could expect my heart to beat after the bypass surgery. He told me the operation was a total success and confidently gave me another 10 years.

Ten more years? Wow! Seemed like a long, long time ahead of me. I calculated; eight years more of flying, plus a couple of years of retired life sounded great! The only thing that worried me was that I did not have a nest egg accumulated for my family after me.

After the recovery room, I was wheeled to the ICU. Dr Mandke came over one more time to see me before leaving for the day. He was trailed by a couple of junior doctors and two nurses. I blame the drugs and the anesthesia, but I blurted out a question that had been niggling at me since before the surgery, "Doctor, please tell me, did I need the surgery, or did you need the money?"

Dr Mandke was stunned, but he realized I was heavily sedated. He came back with his return volley. "Have you seen my new villa? Somebody has to pay for it, young man! Your heart is in the right place. Thank you for your generosity." The junior doctors and nurses had a good laugh, but I could not even chuckle – it hurt to laugh. Dr. Mandke noted my wince with a smug grin. With great dignity, he left the ICU. I thought I had lost my cardiologist and the very best heart surgeon in India, forever. He had just saved my life, and I had questioned his motives. But an hour later, his doctor anesthesiologist wife who had been there for the entire heart surgery procedure, apologized to me for her husband's remark about the villa. "We have no villa. We live in a flat," she explained. She was charming, very compassionate and understanding. Now I blamed her, thinking maybe she had messed up and given me an extra dose of anesthesia, which is why I spoke to her husband the way I did. But I just mumbled, "It's okay. I don't have a villa, too," and hoped the ceasefire truce had been made.

I was in a lot of pain. My chest seemed scorched and felt as if there was a huge rock on top of it. My entire left leg hurt, and it felt like a hive of bees were continually stinging me. I did not know that my surgeon had lacerated, removed, and again stitched up three feet of my vein from my left leg and two feet of veins or arteries from either side of my chest. The stitches were of real cat guts (which got infected two weeks after I was discharged. I was back in hospital where the stitches were removed and restitched. With different cat guts, I hoped). My sternum bone and my ribs were clipped together with six metal clips. I did not know it then, but the clips would set alarms ringing at airport security checks, and I had to show them a certificate from the doctor and Hinduja Hospital that carried a waiver. Dr Mrs Mandke increased the painkillers in my system and sedated me enough to relax my body and mind.

I dozed off for many hours. Between waking up and dozing off, it was very comforting to see my Maloo, Zeena, Jennifer, Mehernosh in turns, one at a time. A personal, special ICU nurse stayed round the clock by my side.

The next day it seemed as if I had bounced back a bit, but the pain continued to be excruciating. There was a continuous stream of Air India friends visiting me. I spun a story to some of them to give me some hundred-rupee notes to tip the ward boys. Very soon, I had a stack of hundred-rupee notes. In the afternoon, I managed to bribe a ward boy who was mopping the floor. I addressed him as 'Dikra Ramu' and asked him to purchase a couple of strips of Brufen 600s for me with the hundred-rupee notes I had stashed. I did not know that ward boys dispensed medical advice, too. He sidled closer to me and mumbled that Brufen 600 would not cut it. What I needed was some ganja and he would be happy to procure some for me. I was tempted, oh so tempted! But I disappointed Ramu by sticking with Brufen 600. Two hours later, I swallowed a handful of painkillers, Brufen 600s. I was on cloud nine, and the rock from my chest had lifted.

I must have been on a high. The same evening, I slipped out of the ICU pushing a steel stand on wheels holding the saline bottle, to meet all my family members in the guest waiting room. This caused a bit of a 'dhamaal', excitement inside and outside the ICU, but I was thrilled to see all my family at the same time. But I came down to earth when, two days later, I had internal bleeding due to the Brufen.

Soon I heard that they put up a big notice on different Air India office noticeboards that no one was allowed to visit me in the hospital as I was very hyper and overactive. That put a dampener on my social life in the hospital.

A week later, around mid-afternoon, on 12th March 1993, I was discharged from the hospital.

A truly history making date for discharge: at around the same time I was being driven in the ambulance from Hinduja hospital in Mahim to Kalina, a series of bomb blasts were rocking Bombay, at various locations. Hotels, office buildings, banks, petrol pumps and markets were bombed and blasted. A series of twelve terrorist bombing attacks took place on that day in Bombay. Two hundred and fifty-seven people were killed, and another fourteen hundred injured and hospitalized. A total of 13 RDX car bombs with shrapnel had been used. It was the darkest and saddest day for Bombayites.

The Almighty blessed my family and me. I survived a heart attack while driving. I survived ninety per cent blockages, and a triple bypass. And I survived a few strips of Brufen 600 from Dikra Ramu.

Lastly, I survived 13 different RDX bomb blasts while I was in an ambulance on the road, in North Bombay. I later learned that the closest we came to danger was when we drove past Fishermen's Colony, where grenades were thrown.

Looking back thirty years later, I remember that Dr. Mandke had given me a life expectancy of another ten years. It has now been thirty years. I wonder if it is because of my motto:

Khao Piyo Karo Anand

Tel Lagaave Dev Anand.

29

What the Bloody Hell!

Sometimes, among friends, you just have to say a phrase, and everyone knows who you are referring to. It was the same with *What the bloody hell*! If you were among the Air India crowd, everyone knew you were talking about Raj Verma, the in-flight supervisor.

Imagine a matinee idol like Danny Kaye, twirling a cigarette in his slim fingers. Imagine Clark Gable with a cigarette between his lips, talking like Peter Sellers in the movie *The Party*, and making us all laugh the way Charlie Chaplin did in the silent movie era. And you have *What the bloody hell!* - Raj Verma.

Charlie Chaplin made us all roar, laugh and giggle with his mouth 'shut'. Raj Verma made us all grin, chuckle, belly-laugh and scream with his mouth 'open'. His guffaws, antics, unintended whacky spoofs, his famous sayings, and statements were all rolling-on-the-floor-laughing funny.

Allow me to share some of his famous sayings

> *Birds of the feather, sail in the same boat.*
>
> *Open the window, and let the weather come in.*
>
> *I am well, hope you are in the same well.*
>
> *What is your good name?*
>
> *That store is not open today, as it is closed.*
>
> *Shop lifters will be prostituted.*

If you park here, your tyre will be air out.

And saving the best for last:

I caught her underwares, actually, caught us unawares!

When his grandfather passed away, he needed to take a few days off for a *mundan* ceremony – it was customary to shave your head when an elderly person passes away in the family. When Raj Verma had to fill out his leave application form and give the reason for the request, he entered *I have to get my head cut.*

Once, on a layover in Moscow, Raj Verma was shopping in a crystalware showroom with some of the other crew members. Worried that they would finger the delicate crystalware with their clumsy hands and break them, he warned, *Don't touch yourself, ask some staff.* I am not sure if the staff at the showroom would have obliged!

Another time, on arrival at a transit halt on one of his flights, the transit passengers needed to be kept on board and not deplane. The traffic staff on the tarmac standing near the step ladder, gave in-flight supervisor Raj Verma a signal with his hands showing the 'T' sign, which meant *Transit passengers to stay on board.*

Soon the assistant flight purser was seen serving tea to the traffic staff, who were quite surprised by this unexpected, though welcome, *manna* from heaven. In the meanwhile, the transit passengers were being deplaned and climbing into the waiting buses. Most of them had deplaned by the time the traffic staff realized the blunder. Raj Verma was either still fuzzy by the altitude drop or he had misunderstood the 'T' sign. He thought the traffic officer wanted some tea. Instead of announcing *Transit passengers to remain on board,* he had instructed his assistant flight purser to make and serve tea to the traffic staff below!

Sometimes, Raj Verma forgot if he was on the ground in a hotel or on a flight. Once we landed in Rome on different flights. That evening, crew members from all landed flights in Rome met in Raj's hotel suite. The revelry - drinks and music amongst boisterous bonhomie - went on till late in the night and we became a nuisance to the occupants of the neighbouring rooms.

Unable to sleep, some guests complained to the night manager at the hotel, who came to Raj's room and very politely asked us all to please keep it down. We shushed each other and gradually the noise level was dialed down.

Suddenly, we jumped out of our skins, when someone bellowed, "Hey guys, carry on, enjoy, don't worry about the noise. Carry on the *dhamaal*, I will sign for it, enjoy!!" It was Raj Verma. He still thought he was up in the air and all he had to do as in-flight supervisor was to follow regulations and countersign all flight reports, any bar items, dry stores, any other uplift requisitions, any breakages, any in-flight problems, any untoward incidences, etc! When our hearts stopped racing and we had climbed back into our skins, we had to remind him that he was back on ground.

I could go on at great length, regaling my readers about Raj's ridiculously amusing, hilariously funny remarks, comments, and malapropisms. He was a wonderful man and a beautiful human being - loveable, amiable, cheery, happy, and upbeat.

Let me end with saying that Raj has passed on to his abode in the sky – the skies he loved flying. I would like to think that he is keeping other departed souls frolicking with laughter.

God bless his soul!

30

Magic Words: Yatha Ahu Vario & Ashem Vohu

These days we live in a world where every faith and every tenet of faith is tested. We are surrounded by words flung at us that try to define who we are: believer, non-believer, atheist, agnostic, evangelist, godless, infidel – the list goes on and on. In the midst of this roiling cacophony, one needs to have a deep-rooted internal belief and faith that gives you a few words that tether you to all the goodness the universe holds for you.

For me it is: "Yatha Ahu Vairyo" and "Ashem Vohu."

My mother had sublime faith in her Parsi prayers and made us repeat these five words over and over: "Yatha Ahu Vairyo" and "Ashem Vohu."

Earlier in this book, I have narrated the events of 1946 and 1947.

In the days before the India-Pakistan partition, ruthless and barbaric riots were the order of the day. Killings, blood baths and massacres, murder and rape, arson and carnage broke out on the streets, lanes, and bye-lanes of our beautiful winter town of Shimla. The city had become red hot, smouldering with blazing flames, due to senseless rioting between Hindus, Muslims, and Sikhs. Everyone was mercilessly slaughtering and annihilating everyone else who belonged to a different faith, a different religion.

My parents, my elder brother, my elder sister and I, escaped from Shimla by the skin of our teeth. It was nothing short of a miracle.

We survived the journey from Shimla to Bombay with only the clothes on our backs, and we travelled by different modes of transport to reach Bombay. There was danger and threats, peril and uncertainty, menace and crisis lurking everywhere around us.

What kept us moving was a constant soft, sweet and gentle chant from my brave mother's lips every minute, every hour, every day, every night, and specially whenever danger loomed close to us. What kept us moving ahead was my father's faith in his sharp mind, his mental and physical strength, and his loaded 12 bore rifle.

I was five years old. "Yatha Ahu Vairyo" and "Ashem Vohu" were magic words to me, just like my father delivering the words "Aabra Ka Dabra," while performing his tricks for me. I did not know the rest of the magic words. I saw that every time we recited these words, we felt a bit better, a bit more protected, a bit more secure. Those five words calmed and soothed my young mind.

During our escape, whenever my father was stopped, confronted, and questioned, we gleaned that those five words made us feel safe, courageous, and stronger inside. Much later, my mother told us that we were on the road for more than two weeks before we finally reached Bombay Central Railway station – the whole family alive and in one piece. We must have repeated these words silently in our minds and murmuring on our lips a million times.

I do believe, even today if I or my loved ones are in a spot of trouble, these five words make the trouble go away. Such is the power of prayer.

When we stayed in my grandmother's cottage in Vakola, Santacruz east, my mom and I were going to visit our uncle, Vicajee, in Dadar. We stood, holding hands, and waiting for a train to pass by before the railway track gate would swing open, and we could go across to the other side of the tracks. Suddenly at a distance, I saw a running train turning around the bend and coming straight towards us.

I remembered Shimla. I froze. Then I don't know what came over me. I snatched my hand from my mother's grip and ran across the railway track to the other side. I don't know which sound was louder – the train whistle or my mother's scream. Seconds later, the train divided my mother from me. I was on the other side, alone and shaking.

Those Shimla images were flashing through my mind's eye. Along with that came the memory of my mother's murmuring lips: "Yatha Ahu Vairyo" and "Ashem Vohu." Instinctively, I recited the words with my eyes closed; those five words tripping over each other to keep up with my racing heart.

The train thundered past. When I opened my eyes, my mother stood on the other side, with her hand on her heart and her lips, not murmuring, but shouting the same five words in terror. She raced across the tracks, lifted me up and hugged me. When she kissed me over and over again, her tears fell on my cheeks, and our tears mingled both in love and fear.

Once again, those magic words worked for me. For us.

My faith grew stronger, and it was tested many times.

In my grandma's cottage in Vakola, we had to walk a hundred steps to answer nature's call. Away from the main home, there were two raised toilets with a tin roof and tin doors. There was no flush, no toilet seats, no toilet paper, and no bum washers – only a bucket of water under a running tap and a mug. The stone flooring was raised with a huge bucket under it, to collect the human waste and would be changed and replaced every afternoon.

An earlier story tells of my horror when I slipped and fell into the over filled bucket, chest high. I was stuck and couldn't move. I started crying and sobbing, hoping to be rescued. When I had no more tears, I remembered the magic words, "Yatha Ahu Vairyo" and "Ashem Vohu." I repeated them a few times and miraculously, my sister, Lily, was there. Lily was always my guardian angel. She slid open the stopper of the tin door with a fine stick and rescued me.

The next thing I knew, I was in the bathing room of the house. Lily was spraying me and dousing me with a hose pipe, for a long time, while I kept murmuring those magic words over and over again.

A year passed by, and I was six years old. We had shifted into our new home in Nana Chowk on Grant Road. That five-storey building 'Motta Mansion' still stands there like a rock. I see it often while passing by. That building had an inverted U-shaped road around it. Our immediate and next door neighbour's on the fifth floor were the Harda family, and their children, Neville and Mehli Harda became my childhood friends. Later they also became In-flight supervisors in Air India with me. We have remained good friends even through the Covid rampage.

As kids, the three of us would sit on the footpath outside our building entrance and wait with a pile of small stones and pebbles. Every time a car drove by, we would take turns to throw some stones at it. That was our daily game, our entertainment, and our fun.

One day, it was my turn to throw stones. I took aim at a passing black car and threw. My stone hit the windshield of the car. It screeched to a halt. The owner reversed the car. Mehli and Neville scrambled up and ran through the building entrance and sprinted up all the way to the 5th floor. I tried to run, but my legs froze.

The car door opened, and the owner got out. He had an angry scowl on his red face.

My face became ash grey; and, to my embarrassment, I felt a warm dribble seep down my squatted legs. I was peeing in my pants. My 'soo-soo', trickled from between my legs, along the footpath, down to the road. Without a thought, I started babbling, "Yatha Ahu Vairyo" and "Ashem Vohu."

The enraged owner strode straight up to me. He stopped. He noticed my ashen face and the trail of my fear from my wet pants. Without a word, he got back in his car and drove off.

Saved again, by those five magic words!

My mother also taught me the importance of another six words. "Good thoughts, good words, good deeds." They were the basis, doctrine, and foundation of our Zoroastrian religion. To be a good Parsi, I had to follow the basic principles, endorsed in those six words.

I can say, with honesty, that I have followed those basic principles in my life.

31

The Sacred Fires of Udvada and Lonavala

Every faith has its beliefs and in an ideal world, mankind works together to weave a tapestry of understanding, accommodation, and inclusive environment for peaceful co-existence of all faiths. During my lifetime I have been blessed to witness all the good that man is bestowed with.

Several centuries ago, Persia consisted of Iran, Iraq, and a few other countries. Around thirteen hundred years ago, in the eighth century, Zoroastrian Persians were being persecuted by the Arabs who had taken over their country by defeating the prosperous Sasanian Empire. The Arabs tried to coerce the Parsis to give up their Zoroastrian faith and embrace Islam.

In order to preserve their faith, save their religion, and their holy fire, our forefathers escaped from Persia and sailed away to different countries. Some boats sailed to Germany and others came to India.

The very devout religious Zoroastrian Parsis who fled in their boats across the Arabian sea reached the shores of western India and landed on the beautiful beaches of Sanjan, a port in Gujarat. They carried their sacred fire with them: 'Atash' called Iranshah, the symbol of Light and Ahura Mazda.

At the time they landed, Jadhav Rana was the king and ruler of the land, and was very concerned about the newcomers who landed on the shores of his kingdom. They did not speak the same language; the newcomers spoke Farsi. How was he to communicate his concern to them? After much thought, King Rana sent his messenger to the Persians with a bowl brimming with milk; to demonstrate that his kingdom was already replete with his own people and could not accommodate the newcomers.

The Zoroastrian priest understood the message. He took the bowl of milk back to the king and took with him a bowl of sugar. Bit by bit, he added sugar to the bowl and stirred it with care and patience. The sugar dissolved and the milk was sweetened, made delicious and richer, but did not overflow.

King Jadhav Rana understood the priest. The Parsis from Persia would assimilate and intermingle with the Indian community and make the land richer and sweeter with their high values and hard work. He was very impressed with this gesture and welcomed them into the land, offered them many welcome gifts, and helped them to settle in the kingdom of Gujarat.

The Parsis, a miniscule minority, with their strong and pious beliefs, honesty, and business acumen, settled, blended, and assimilated very well into the Indian community, like 'sugar in the milk'. Their core beliefs were good thoughts, good words and good deeds. Bai Motlibai Maneckjee Wadia of Bombay sponsored the building of the current temple in Udvada in 1742. Our original sacred fire, the Iran Shah Atash Behram, was housed here. Thus, Udvada is the holiest of the holy lands for the Parsis and Iranis.

There were still Zoroastrian Persians in other countries, like Yemen. In 1967, the British left Yemen and the country embraced a hardcore communist system of governance. For the thirteen Parsi families settled in Aden in Yemen, it became increasingly difficult to protect their temple and sacred fire. The communist government wanted to seize their temple.

To preserve their religion and sacred fire, the families decided to move the 'live burning fire' to another country. The government of India agreed to be their host country. But the dilemma was a physical one: how does one move a live sacred fire across countries?

International and political opinions of the Parsi community in India and Aden were sought and discussed at great length. Finally, it was arranged that Air India would send a Boeing 707 aircraft, manned by an all Parsi crew, with Parsi priests and other Parsi escorts to receive the sacred 'Atash' fire from Aden and bring it to India.

On the fourteenth of November 1976, an all Parsi crew, including the pilot, Air India Captain Sam Pedder took off from Santacruz Airport in Bombay for Aden. We all know smoking is strictly prohibited in all the airlines of the world due to the fire hazard to the aircraft and danger to the lives on board. An incredible effort was being made to fly a 'live burning fire' in a pressurized cabin at thirty thousand feet. The first ever incident in the world of this kind; history was being made!

The aircraft landed at Santacruz Airport at 7:00 am Everyone heaved a sigh of relief when the fire, treated with all the love, care, benevolence, and warmth (literally) reached Bombay, safe and secure, in less than four hours. It was given a ceremonial welcome: fed with sandalwood and chants of 'Yatha Ahu Variyo,' and 'Ashem Vohu'. The mobeds - Zoroastrian clerics - who fed the live fire did the 'Padyab Kushti' and 'Atash Niyaesh', and other prayers.

The Atash Padsha was then taken to the Soonawala Agiary in Mahim by a special luxury bus. After resting the live fire for a few hours, around 1:30pm, the holy fire commenced the second phase of its journey, to its new home at Adenwala Agiary, in Lonavala.

The scenic winding roads across the hills and ghats from Bombay to Lonavala was teeming with devout Parsis and Iranis. A procession of seventy to eighty cars, and motorbikes as long as the eye could see, followed the sacred fire. In addition, there were eight airconditioned luxury buses with Parsi drivers, carrying many other Parsis and Iranis, who did not want to be left out of this faith-affirming experience.

With due ceremonies and prayers, the 'Atash Padsha' was installed in the specially created domain right next to the sacred fire of the Lonavala Adenwala Agiary. The Agiary thronged with avid and ardent Zoroastrian devotees. Amidst solemn piety, the air resonated with gleeful merriment and congratulatory shouts of joy. The Parsis and Iranis thumped each other on the backs; only the Bawas would even dare to dream up a scheme like this and execute it! And successfully too! Rules and dangerous government regimes do not apply to a community that makes up its mind to break the rules!

Another historic milestone achieved. The original Atash Padsha was first consecrated at Aden in Yemen in 1883 in Adenwala Agiary. Ninety-three long years later, in 1976, the sacred fire was airlifted and transferred 'live' and was safely installed in the Adenwala Agiary in Lonavala.

32

Married Six Times to the Same Woman!

In her lifetime she was married eight times, to seven men. Are you sure she knew how to count? Must have been weak in math, but strong in men. Ah, but I am talking of Elizabeth Taylor. Not sure if she was good in math, but her beauty captivated millions on the silver screen. She was known to fall in love at the blink of an eye. She married Richard Burton in 1964, divorced him 10 years later in 1974, and remarried him a year later in 1975. That is how the math works out. Married eight times, to seven men.

I'm no Elizabeth Taylor, but in this one regard I came close to breaking her record. Married six times. No, not to seven women, but to the same woman. The love of my life, Meherangiz, fondly called Maloo.

Maloo and I were in love for three years before we got married. Our parents and families were very happy for us. I am a Parsi and Maloo is Bahai – both of Zoroastrian faith. So we could get married according to the Parsi rites, since Maloo's Navjote was done when she was seven-years-old. Navjote is where one is inducted into the Zoroastrian faith. My parents believed, "once a Parsi, always a Parsi" and my father believed that the first marriage is really the only one that counted. He wanted us to be married by Parsi rites. Maloo's parents wanted a Bahai wedding.

In order to keep everyone happy, we decided on an elaborate process.

We had a registered civil marriage at 10:30 am on the 11th February 1966.

The Bahai wedding took place an hour and a half later at 12:00 pm on the 11th February 1966. Mrs Zena Sorabjee performed the Bahai rites.

The Parsi wedding ceremony was held at 6:00 pm in Juhu, since Parsi weddings were only held in the evening.

The three-wedding day was followed by dinner, which was attended by our immediate families, relatives, and close friends.

So, we got closer to Elizabeth Taylor's records by a count of three by the end of the day on 11th February 1966.

But the celebrations did not stop there. The next day, we had a gala buffet dinner reception at the Ambassador Hotel Roof Garden off Marine Drive in Churchgate. The entire staff from Air India Cargo and Traffic celebrated with us. So did all Central Bank of India head office colleagues of Maloo's. Everyone came with their families to grace the occasion. I can't think of a better way to celebrate the union of two hearts.

The count was now at four. Elizabeth Taylor was in the lead.

My father was the Collector of Central Excise and Customs in Ahmedabad. I think he wanted us to *Collect* wedding celebrations. We, the newly married couple were happy to oblige, as if each celebration strengthened our love even more.

Two days later, we were off to my parents' place - Nawab's Bungalow, in Ahmedabad. My father wanted to host one more wedding banquet for all his and my mother's friends of Parsi Gymkhana, the full staff of his department, a few of our relatives, and some of my close friends from Bombay and Ahmedabad, who had also come to attend the function in Ahmedabad. And of course, their families in

Ahmedabad – no invitation was complete without including every member of the family.

We had to sit on an elaborately decorated podium in a huge hall and meet and greet hundreds of invitees as they came in to wish and bless us.

"I could do this over and over again." I whispered to Maloo.

She leaned over as if to brush something away from the back of my neck and gave me a sharp pinch. "As long as it is only with me," she said, her smile in place, but her eyes glinting.

So we (p)inched one step closer to Elizabeth Taylor. Number five.

In the intervening years of traveling with Air India and surrounding myself with the joy of raising a family, I lost track of Elizabeth Taylor.

Many years later, my class of 1960 St. Xavier High School, Ahmedabad, arranged our golden jubilee function in Loyola Hall in Ahmedabad. It was a three-day celebration running from 17th to 19th December 2010. My two daughters and their husbands flew down from Bombay to attend our school get together. I was looking forward to it because my birthday was on 18th December and we could have a double celebration. But my classmates and their wives made it a triple celebration. They threw one more wedding ceremony for us! They went the whole nine yards – complete with garlands, vermillion tikas, rose bouquets, barfis and jalebis (Indian sweets). They even brought in a Catholic priest to pray and bless us.

Marriage number six!

Even with us nipping at her heels with six marriages, Elizabeth Taylor won in the end. But I am exceedingly happy to mention that our daughters, Zeena and Jennifer, together with their husbands and our three grandchildren, celebrated their parents' and their grandparents' golden anniversary at the banquet hall in the Taj at the Gateway of India, Mumbai.

Our daughters had invited every living family member and friend for the occasion, and the best part of the gala festivity was that everyone turned up. It truly was a dream celebration - dining, wining, singing, dancing, speeches galore - magnificent, marvellous, memorable and totally sublime.

The love of my life

33

My mobile, my Digital World!!

Until a few years ago, kindly grandfathers would lift their grandchildren onto their laps while reading the newspaper, only to see the child lean forward and swipe the page as if the newspaper was an iPad or tablet. At other times, they would watch the child pick up a hard bound book and turn it over and inside out to figure out where to plug in the charger.

I had my own Google: An entire hard bound set of Encyclopedia Britannica. These books were a collection of pride and honour in the living room, and an envy of many who visited us.

As for our Google maps, they were the instructions given by strangers on the roadside. In the 60s, 70s and 80s when we were on the road in our family car, we did not feel ignorant to ask for directions. Neither was it wrong to stop our car off the country road, or village lane, and ask strangers for directions. In fact, we felt like stylish city-born folks - like tourists from another world. And our Google maps humans were the kindest, most helpful people we ever met.

From humans, we advanced to folding road maps. An 8"x4" road map unfolded and opened into 4'x2', spread across the laps of the driver and the passenger. It had its own place of pride in the car - the glove compartment.

It seemed so smart to stop the car on the side of the road and unfold the elongated road map on the hood or trunk of the car to find out where on earth we were in the first place, and then decide where to go. Little urchins would sidle up and stand on tip toe and study the map very intently as if they could see themselves on the map.

Today Google takes the fun out of driving down unknown and silent pathways. We always know where we are, where to go, the best route to take, and when we will get to our final destination.

Earlier I had mentioned about the first radio in Motamai cottage being the size of a small suitcase. When I bought my first television, it was the size of a very large suitcase. As large as a steamer trunk, in fact. And when I got my first phone connection, the instrument got a privileged spot in the living room. We had to sit on the chair next to it and talk, after which we wiped the handset reverently, as if wiping off fingerprints after a bank heist.

A TV remote was unheard of and unnecessary, because we got only one channel – Doordarshan – a government funded channel. That too had only an evening broadcast, not an all-day broadcast. A TV remote became a necessity when Doordarshan started its second channel. *The Times They Are a-Changin'* we sang!

Televisions had to be nudged out of their perch to make way for large desktop computers.

Twenty-two years ago, when I retired, I bought a desktop computer. It was such a novelty that I made space for it in the master bedroom. It came with a family of its own: a huge computer table, fitted with lots of shelves, divided into compartments for the accompanying hardware and some software. Vacant shelves and open spaces were designed to seat the twin speakers (the larger the better), family photographs in ornate frames, 'the system' which contained the innards of the operation encased in a metal box, an elongated, retractable keyboard holder, a couple of open compartments with trays for A4 paper and other stationaries, and, an empty shelf for an 'add-on' printer.

My computer table and over-stuffed cushioned revolving chair, additional wall brackets and shelves for a dictionary, different volumes of 'Internet guide for idiots', CDs, DVDs, a crystal bowl, some additional picture frames of the kids and other paraphernalia, took up half the real estate of my bedroom – without paying rent!

When I saw my grandchildren using their iPad, their laptops and computers like they were an extension of their bodies and an intrinsic part of their growing up, I felt illiterate, mindless and unschooled. When they burrowed into their computers and performed magic, I felt very ancient. My children and my grandchildrens' digital world, their expertise, their speed and agility in handling the computer, was nothing less than wizardry for me.

Refusing to leave me behind, and dragging me along in the digital revolution, my daughters gifted me an Apple Macbook with 'built-in' everything. I accepted it happily, not because it was an Apple, but because of the space saving! Suddenly my bedroom opened up when I gave away the extended family that came with the desktop computer.

Before I could even get used to the Apple Macbook, my wife bought me an iPhone. A few months later, I switched to a Samsung smart phone. Memories are short. Like a fickle lover, I soon forgot whatever little I had learned on my desktop computer and laptop. My Samsung mobile became my digital world. (Sorry, Steve Jobs!)

I realise that today every man and woman on the street owns a mobile phone and carries it around 24/7. They use it as an extension of their arm. I came into the game later than them, forewarned and armed, but my Samsung mobile became an extension of my arm, too. I am so comfortable with my little mobile phone, that my unused and uncharged laptop lies neglected in a corner of the house.

My left palm held my 1000+ contacts, my family and friends, my WhatsApp list, my email, my Gmail, my day, my date, my time, my alarm, my music, my on-line bank, and all the breaking news of the world.

And my right hand? What did it do? My right index finger typed an entire book from start to finish - 50,000+ words - on my little Samsung mobile phone!

An entire book on a Samsung Galaxy A 71.

My grandchildren were amused and amazed and, (I would like to think) secretly proud of me. My daughters tell me I may have achieved some sort of a world record by writing and publishing a book with just one finger on my mobile phone and deserve a mention in the Guinness Book of Records!

And me? I am happy that my Samsung Galaxy A 71 gave me the opportunity to take my stories to the world.

34

In Memory of the Old Air India Colony

My dear Farshosh,

Last night I dreamt that I was in our Old Air India Colony 29/6. You and many of our young friends were dancing and rocking to the music pouring from our old Garrard turntable through our monstrously huge, pulsating, and throbbing speakers.

In the centre of the living room, Tehempton Ghaswala, our very own local Tom Jones, was playing his umbrella-cum-guitar, and singing in his high-pitched scratchy voice:

> *Well, I'm your Venus*
> *I'm your fire, at your desire*
> *Well, I'm your Venus*
> *I'm your fire, at your desire*

Except that he kept saying

> *I'm your fire, your misfire!*

Venus! The dream was so very real. I happily travelled back to those ancient and bygone days. The 1970s! The rise of disco! It was all so delightfully engaging, and exciting.

It was very sad to wake up this morning. I was disappointed to find none of you there and wanted to burrow back into my dreams and float back in time. We were very fortuitous to have some very interesting, hilarious, and fascinating friends, and comic characters in our lives.

Do you remember of Tehempton Ghaswala, aka Tom Jones? And do you remember his heartthrob - the very young and very beautiful Camelia, who used to live in the opposite building? Our duplicate Tom Jones would sing 'Delilah' with throbbing passion, zeal, rage, and knife in hand with all his body movements, through our bedroom window. He would replace the name Delilah, with "Camilliaaaaahhh!"

How are you, my dearest Farshosh? How are Pritti and Zubin?

My love to all at home. Now that Covid is on its way out, let us meet sometime and catch up.

Noshir

We lived in the Old Air India Colony at Kalina, Santacruz East in Bombay. In building #29, ground floor, apartment #6 in the heart of the tri-shaped building. Our apartment was famously called "29/6."

It even housed my military green Jawa motorcycle. When I had to leave on extended foreign postings, I would ride full throttle and take it indoors into the hallway by riding and jumping up five stairway steps, right into the living room through the passage.

I also had a yellow, ten horsepower, American 'Indiana' bike. It was majestic, magnificent, and colossal. It betrayed me when it caught fire while I was riding it with a full tank of fuel on the peripheral airport road. I gave it away to my brother-in-law Dara, but he too could not get it back on the road. Sadly, it had to be scrapped.

But what clearly distinguished me as a Parsi was my first love: my two-door sea green Standard Herald with a double red band, across its length. We had installed a fire extinguisher, an emergency glass window breaking hammer, a fixed torch, a rotating fan on the dashboard, shiny door guards, lights, a music system with surround speakers, glowing reflectors, floating compasses, and musical horns. My car was a moving accessory showroom!

29/6 was our home; our 24/7 restaurant, nightclub, discotheque, pub, temple. For our two daughters, it was their alma mater. 29/6 is where we all grew up. We laughed, hollered, rejoiced, sighed, danced, played, and lived our life fully - Marlboro style. To our very intimate friends, it was a den. To us, it was *home sweet home* for eighteen years! From 1967 to 1985! But it seemed like we lived several lifetimes there.

Young and close friends from the neighbourhood, Air India colleagues and some very special and entertaining *time-pass* visitors dropped in to make our evenings more entertaining and more enjoyable than watching any hilarious movie. And the weekends! Ah, the weekends with loud music, dancing, laughter, joy, and celebrations. We would listen to music on full blast with the volume knob turned to the max. Everyone's favourites were Boney M, Michael Jackson, Tom Jones, Engelbert Humperdinck, Elvis Presley, Boy George, Shirley Bassey, Diana Ross, Barbra Streisand, Neil Diamond, and the list goes on and on. As the sun went down, we would get up from our chairs - one by one - slowly, casually, glass in hand, to the rock and throb of the loud beat. With a few pints of beer or scotch on the rocks under our belt, we would dance the night away.

The neighbours would exclaim with bonhomie, "The Sanjanas have begun!" If the music went on way past midnight, the neighbours who were being deprived of sleep anyway would come over without invitation and join the band. "If you can't beat them, join them," was the motto! And they were welcomed into the Sanjana fold.

We laughed, we partied, we ate lobsters, English pork, king prawns, black and golden yellow Russian caviar from the Caspian Sea, Chello kebabs from Iran, tenderloin steaks and sautéed potatoes, cheesecake from Frankfurt, kind courtesy the catering manager, Carlos Wadia. We also enjoyed Thai, Chinese, Indian, and Parsi cuisine. Parsi specialties included Dhansakh - spiced Parsi dal with brown rice, Sali-Boti - boneless mutton with thin strips of deep-fried potatoes, Patra ni macchi - baked fish in green chutney wrapped in banana leaves, and lagan nu custard - a special sweet custard, prepared specially for Parsi weddings.

We drank many different wines: French, German and sometimes Indian. We had white wines, red wines, port wine, Scotch, Black Label, Chivas Regal, Smirnoff vodka, Heineken beer, an occasional champagne, and even Dom Perignon on very special occasions.

Those were also the very early days of my flying job in Air India. Though it is now thirty-six years since we bid adieu to our beautiful and awesome Old Air India Colony, I remember, very clearly, each and every neighbour of ours in that building and some other buildings around us.

On these pages, I would like to recollect many faces in our Air India Staff Colony.

The Vijay Goel: He was a head clerk, though very young, in the Air India training school centre, In-flight Service Department. A regular visitor to 29/6. He believed he was the reincarnation of Bruce Lee. He enthralled us all with his Kung Fu moves and shadow boxing in which his high and wild kicks in the air often ripped his tight pants at the... you know where.

His usual question was, "How's The Maloo?" to which I would reply, "How's The Vijay?" which is what got him his name *The Vijay Goel*. Once when Maloo had undergone a dual operation, removing her gall bladder and her appendix, The Vijay came with my best friend Ramesh Angle to Parsi General Hospital. While Ramesh was trying to locate Maloo's private room, The Vijay approached the nurses' station and inquired, "Where's The Maloo?"

Sukhbir Thakur: Air India Senior Manager In-flight-Supervisor, Sukhbir Thakur, was the kindest man the kids had ever known. My daughters loved him immensely. He often prepared breakfast for them and his own lovely daughter, Shonali, treating them like first class passengers and giving them the feel of sitting in first class. Sukhbir was also like a magnet to all the children in and around our building #29.

He was famous for his newly dug up trenches in his garden in case of bombings from enemy planes during the India-Pakistan war and would pace up and down with his loaded air gun.

Sukhbir loved his new Lambretta scooter and claimed it moved like the wind. It had special license plates: 747. He would often state, "Every nut-bolt in my ruddy scooter is imported!" Like the 747, maybe?

Chandu Kaltak: He was a very active committee member of our Air India Colony 'society stores.' He was a very fast talking, small made, funny guy. All his conversations started and ended with a high five saying, "The name is Chandu Kaltak. Why fear when I'm here? Taali!" Another high five.

Derrick Brian: Derrick was an intensely passionate and enthusiastic tropical fish lover and small-time breeder. He was known in all the mom-and-pop local pet fish shops as the "Singapore Wala, angel fish and guppy breeder." He used his 'free and ninety per cent' concessional tickets from Air India every year to fly to Singapore and bring back gravid and fully loaded trio-guppies, prize winning fighter fish, and angel fish to breed and to sell. He always started and finished his conversation with, "Wohhhh jo guppy! Wohhhh Fighterrrrrr!"

Mr. Sampath: He was the head security officer and our next-door neighbour, but he didn't offer much security.

I had beaten up two guys for eve-teasing and pulling the plaits of my daughter's domestic help, Gracie. Late in the evening, some Vakola *gundaas* (hooligans, troublemaker gangs, from nearby Vakola) laid siege to my house. They came as a gang, congregated outside our building, abusing and shouting my name and daring me to come out. I expected Mr. Sampath to come out and handle them, but during the sudden onslaught and the fracas that followed with stone pelting on our grilled windows, the lights of Mr. Sampath's apartment were switched off suddenly as if the family had gone to bed.

The next morning when we told him of the previous night's incident, he roared, "Array, you should have woken me up. I would have removed their skin and put salt on it!" In the darkness of his house, he may have removed my skin and put salt on it!

Mrs. Lakhpatti: She was cute, roly-poly, and chubby, and lived three doors away. She was always found "reeeeelaxing" the whole day, in a zen-like state with her arms stretched out up and above her head. We played tennis-ball cricket in the front side of our building, with her sons, Ashok and Fardoo. The biggest problem was to get Fardoo out.

Sabberwals: The spiritual and righteous Sabbberwals lived in the apartment directly above ours. Their unmarried daughter, Jaya, was a great devotee of the very popular yet fake Sai Maharaj, not to be mistaken with the great saint 'Shirdi ke Sai Baba.'

Jaya was a very close friend of my daughters. They were invited every week on Thursdays, to participate in the bhajan and prayer service upstairs. I think they went mainly for the goodies - the prasad and the mithai laid out after the prayer service.

The Morgans: Danny and Antoinette were our nicest, best, and closest friends and neighbours. Their very special and differently abled daughter, Anne would always sit at our doorstep, untangling bundles of strings and threads. When the Morgans immigrated to Canada, we were heart broken.

Richard Coelho: Sr. Check Flight Purser, Richard Coelho and his wife Cissy lived two doors away on the other side, with their fun-loving son Dicky, and his very sweet sister Audrey. Richard had the unique knack of remembering everyone's birthdays, and never failing to wish them, whichever part of the world they were in.

There are some of the sad memories.

Srinivasans: Shrini, as I used to address him very lovingly, his most jovial wife Leela, her wonderful brother Ramu, their two children Anuradha and Ashok (my daughters' classmates) remain our best friends even today. We shared a birthday: 18th December.

But the saddest catastrophe and misfortune overtook Shrini.

On 31st May 1981, there was an attempted sabotage on the Air India Boeing 707, 'Makalu', which was earmarked to fly prime minister Mrs Indira Gandhi on a foreign diplomatic tour. The control cables of the plane were almost cut. There were cries of foreign terrorist involvement, that lead to a spate of arrests in Air India. Mr. Srinivasan, the director and head of the security department at Nariman Point was made the scapegoat. This very honest, faultless, and innocent man had to bear the brunt of the witch hunt. He lost his job and the stress of the situation soon led to health issues and, eventually, his death.

Ramesh Angle: Ramesh was the greatest friend anyone could ever hope for. His loving family consisted of his dear wife Aruna, his son Rohit, a brilliant university topper and his very beautiful daughter Rupali. In the senior years of his life, he lost Aruna to multiple onslaughts of cancer. Soon after, he also lost his darling, young daughter Rupali due to her fragile and weakened lungs.

Losing Ramesh was one of the big tragedies of my life. I miss him the most.

Before I die, it is my desire to visit, at least once, my apartment 29/6, to see our garden once again with the huge mango tree that my wife 'The Maloo' planted fifty years ago.

I would like to end with this story the way it was narrated to me, because I never had the pleasure of joining the two lovely ladies on their jaunts.

One was the love of my life. My wife, Maloo.

The other was Mrs. Mahalakshmi Sen. She had lost her husband and lived with her son and daughter in the adjoining building in the Old Air India staff colony in Santacruz East. She was also Maloo's shopping companion. No, reverse that – Maloo was her shopping companion, because whenever Mrs. Sen needed to go shopping, she would always request her closest friend, Maloo, to accompany her in her car to Bandra on 'Hill' road.

They always visited one particular roadside shop, selling sugarcane outside the Elco shopping centre in Bandra. Initially Maloo placed an order for sugarcane juice with ice.

"Ask for it without ice," Mahalakshmi whispered to her.

"But I want mine with ice," Maloo said, in her normal tone. "It is hot."

"Shhh! Just do! I'll explain later," came the whispered instruction.

Intrigued, Maloo was a good student and waited for her next instructions.

"Take a few sips," said Mahalakshi.

Maloo did, without complaining about the warm sugarcane juice. Where was her ice?

After a few gulps, Mahalaksmi held out her glass towards the vendor for crushed ice. Maloo also held out her glass, thinking, "See, I told you we need ice." But the mystery was solved when they walked away from the vendor and Mahalaksmi told her with a triumphant grin, "See, this way we get more juice. At least quarter glass extra!"

The ladies walked away as if they had won the lottery.

On other shopping visits, they did the same at Elco Snack Bar in Bandra. Here, it was not sugarcane juice but Falooda; and only Mahalakshi won the lottery, because Maloo was diabetic and could not have Falooda. For the uninitiated, Falooda is a delicious drink with sweetened rose syrup, chia seeds, milk and ice cream. Maloo ordered a cappuccino coffee without sugar, instead.

Mahalakshmi always ordered two half glasses of Falooda. When the waiter was out of earshot, Mahalakshmi leaned across the table and like a conspirator, explained to Maloo that ordering two half glasses of Falooda, gets you more in quantity than one full glass.

"Always order two halves, instead of one full, for the price of one," she instructed Maloo.

When the waiter returned with one sizzling hot cappuccino and two half glasses of Falooda, Mahalakshmi would ask for additional crushed ice in a separate bowl which she added to the two half glasses of Falooda, filling them to the brim. She now had two glasses of Falooda.

Mahalakshmi loved one upmanship and drank her Falooda with a twinkle in her eye.

At the end, they always left a generous tip for the waiter.

In our house it became a joke. "You should have asked for two half-husbands," I teased Maloo. "Then you would have got quarter extra husband."

To that, Maloo would retort, "I didn't even ask for one half-husband, and see what a treasure I got. I've got the best husband." And we would dance around the living room.

Mrs. Sen had a style of her own. She was one tough lady and had a lot of clout. She worked for Air India at the old airport. The way she carried herself at work, everyone thought she was the Airport Manager and in-charge of everything around her.

However, as a friend she was 'all heart' and always there to lend a helping hand to those in need. She was lovable and full of fun, with a heart of gold – a full heart of gold, not two half hearts of gold!

35

Saaro Maanas: A Good Man

My family has nicknamed me Saaro Maanas, meaning 'a good man.' Contrary to the meaning, the name was bestowed on me because, without exception, I believe and trust each and every one that comes into my life.

You can call me a 'humanist' – I have faith in humanity, believe in the basic goodness of humans, and value each individual at face value. To this end, God has blessed me with all good people in my eighty-two years on this planet. Till date, no one has broken my trust in them.

I neither preach, nor do I teach anyone how to live their life. We have only one life and everyone should live their life the way they want. I do not profess to hold the secrets to a successful, happy, and fulfilled life.

I have lived a very charmed, happy, and fulfilled life; and within my limitations, I have had a very successful life so far. My charmed life started with the most wonderful and loving parents any child could ever hope to have.

My dearest, beloved mother, Jala Nader Sanjana, was the most beautiful, angelic, admirable, kindest, and the most devoted wife and mother that ever walked on Mother Earth.

It is said that *God takes soonest those he loveth best*. God called my mother when she was only fifty-two-years-old. Her passing away was one of the saddest and most grief-stricken day of my life.

My dearest and most honourable father, Nader Jehangir Sanjana, was one of the strongest men India had seen in those days. He was a multiple gold and silver medalist wrestler. He was also a courageous and fearless shikari in his younger days. Hunting big cats in the 1920s and 30s was a sport during British Raj. But he never killed for sport.

My father was very well-known as a saviour and a hero to the villagers of Castle Rock in Uttar Kannada. Scores of hapless villagers settled just outside the very dense forests in the Western Ghats, in Uttar Kannada, located in the state of Karnataka. They shared the forest with man-eating panthers and tigers. These man-eating wild cats would tread very stealthily, stalk the villagers (only humans, never the cattle!), surprise, attack, kill and drag away the poor half-alive victims from the villages close to the impenetrable jungles.

My father would be called urgently by the gram panchayat, to rid the village of these wild animals. It was his mission to make the villages safer places to live in.

My beloved mother became a victim to pleurisy (water formation in the lungs) that led to the third and fourth stage cancer of her lungs.

Just a few years after my mother passed away, my father's health deteriorated very rapidly. In a case of *'from the sublime to the ridiculous!'* he underwent no less than four to five major heart attacks and survived. My father's cardiologist, Dr. Farokh E. Udvadia of Breach Candy Hospital, Bombay, said that in all his years of practicing medicine, my father was the only patient who survived five heart attacks.

Unfortunately, my father succumbed to his sixth major heart attack and passed away, at the age of sixty-four.

My parents are now happy, and they walk with God Almighty! No more pains. No more aches.

My elder brother, Rusi, who is ten years older than me, has always been my mentor and my guiding light. He is one of the nicest brothers anyone can ever hope to have. I owe him a lot for whatever I am today.

My most loving sister, Lily, is my childhood companion and my best friend. Being four years older to me, she was also my protector and childhood guardian. Her getting married at the tender age of seventeen and leaving our family home, felt like the sun setting on a very cold winter evening. Although I was happy for Lily, I was temporarily heartbroken.

God has been very good to me. My wife Maloo and I have been happily married for the last fifty-six years. She has always been the love of my life. She gave me Zeena and Jennifer—two beautiful, compassionate, benevolent, humane, and wonderful daughters in the world. Ten sons could not have done better!

My two daughters gave us two very good-natured, handsome, and successful, fabulous and outstanding sons-in-law, Mehernosh and Serge, and three most awesome, loving, thoughtful, and beautiful grandchildren - Kaizia, Kayan, and Gisele.

What more can my wife and I ask for?

36

Saaro Maanas: A Good Man – The Master Key

As someone who has found and stayed in touch with most of my loving school friends from my early days in St. Xavier's School, Ahmedabad, in the mid-50s, and more than a thousand crew members, ex-colleagues, and friends, from my working years in Air India since 1962, I can say I have a Master Key to love, life and happiness!

Allow me to share it with my readers.

1. Speak no ill of anyone and only speak the good you know of everyone.

2. Eliminate the word 'criticism' from your dictionary and replace it with appreciation and praise.

   Criticism is a put-down. It is unhealthy and leads to provocation. It wounds a person's self-confidence, hurts their sense of self-esteem, and brings on lasting grudges and bitterness.

3. Try to see only the good and the very best in everyone; and tell them so from your heart.

   I see a Saaro Manas in everyone—a good person in every human being I meet, from deep within my heart.

4. Be hearty in your appreciation and lavish in your praise.

   We often take the people in our lives for granted. We seldom let them know how much we appreciate them. The power of appreciation is an immense gift we all possess, and we should use it lavishly.

5. Criticism is like a boomerang. It will always come back to you.

   You will do well to remove the word 'criticism' from your dictionary and see the changes it brings to your life.

6. The Bible says, "Judge not that thou be not judged."

7. Appreciation is a vitamin and nourishment for the soul. It is nourishment for confidence, self-dignity, and for the morale.

   People crave appreciation as much as they crave food. Appreciation is the best vitamin for the soul, as also, for our self-esteem. We nourish our children and our family with good nutritious food, scores of herbal products, vitamins, and medicines for better health, but do we nourish their self-esteem? Do we nourish their confidence, dignity, and morale? Maybe we don't do enough. Give them the appreciation vitamin! Let them not have an appreciation vitamin deficiency.

8. Avoid getting into an argument.

   If you lose it, you lose. If you win it, you will still lose it because you hurt the other person's ego and pride. You will make the other person feel small.

   If you really need to resort to scolding, berating, or admonishing someone during an argument, never do it in public, in front of others. Opinions may differ, but that is no reason to tear into their self-respect. They will always respect you for that and take the correction well.

9. Flattery is a lie. Flattery is hypocritical and insincere.

   Flattery is deceitful. Flattery is a cheap compliment. No

one wants pretense and deception. Pay genuine tribute and offer sincere recognition. The difference between sincere appreciation and blatant flattery is that one comes from the heart, the other comes from a conniving mind. People will remember that for years, even a lifetime.

10. Find the best in people and compliment them on what makes them the best. Everybody loves a genuine compliment.

I am not suggesting you give away accolades and rewards randomly. I am merely suggesting a new approach to life. Very discreetly, look for and find the best in people. It could be their pretty face, their thick locks of hair, their beautiful well-manicured hands and nails, their cheerful and helpful nature, their winsome smile, their thoughtfulness, their honesty, or their humble nature. Everybody loves a compliment that comes from the heart.

11. A person's first name is the sweetest and most alluring sound in the world to them.

When I worked in the Air India cargo department, I called every porter, loader, and head loader by their name. I made a connection and they loved it! I did the same with every baggage handler and peon in the traffic department.

In 1968, when I started flying as a cabin crew member in Air India in-flight service, crew transport drivers would come to pick us up at the most unearthly hours. Most crew members would address them as 'Bhaiya' or 'Beta.' Addressing them as 'Brother' or 'Son' was good, but I made it a point to greet them by their first name. After that, we developed a beautiful rapport. We were one big happy family and regularly enquired about the well-being of each other's family with genuine interest.

When the drivers brought a despatch rider (DR) messenger

message for our signature, we always invited them in for a quick cold drink, a cup of tea, or even a glass of cold water. Offering a cup of tea was like opening our hearts to them and extending our hand in friendship.

A smile and a warm greeting once given never leaves you. It always comes back to you. When you get dressed for the day, the expression you wear on your face is far more important than the shirt on your back. The smile is a forerunner and an emissary of good will.

12. Show complete trust in your comrades and subordinates. They will very, very seldom let you down.

I would put complete trust in all my crew to handle their work. I would hand over the bar keys as well as the bar float money box to my assistant flight purser. I never, ever lost any money. My crew did their very best to see that the correct amount in various currencies came in and out of the cash box. My positivity, my confidence, my conviction, and my trust in my crew proved to be bulletproof and worked like magic.

I carried that trust into my personal life, too. Many a time, I have asked our household help to open a cupboard and bring my wallet. There never has been a problem there either.

13. The Bible says, "Do unto others what you would have others do unto you."

To be able to practice this, is not an easy virtue. But it is absolutely invaluable.

Everyone thinks that the drinks and meal service on a flight is handled with great efficiency. But for the purser, handling the liquor and other sales services and accounting for it with the cash box is a harried activity. A very stressful activity.

All the bar and the various 'Sky bazaar' items, liquor bottles, liquor and liqueur miniatures, wines, champagnes, cigarettes, perfumes, colognes, cosmetics, artificial jewellery, toiletries, and other ancillary items for sale on board the flight was the responsibility of the flight purser. The approximate sales on a normal flight were over thousands of US dollars in various world currencies.

On every flight, the cash box containing various currencies in notes and in change were kept in the purser's personal care. Due to the hurried liquor and bar sales services cut short because of shortage of time air turbulence or other reasons, we pursers would sometimes be out of pocket! We would find the shortfall only after reaching the hotel at the destination or home, after we cross-checked all the currencies against the sales of the flight.

A few pursers kept an eagle eye on their bar and cash collections, since no one wanted to lose hard earned money and pay out of their pocket. But there were other pursers who habitually complained of being out of pocket and showed a loss at the end of each flight. In loud voices, they declared the loss in dollars and pounds, which made the rest of the cabin crew working on that flight very uncomfortable, and humiliated, as if they were being accused of pilfering.

In my thirty-two years of flying, I rarely lost any money in the final tally. If I did, I remained silent about it because it was all a part of the game.

14. Build up the other person's reputation so much and so high that he/she will always want to live up to it.

15. Avoid the three C's as you would avoid a scorpion - criticizing, complaining, and condemning.

    Not following these three 'C's brings on a fourth 'C' - complications.

16. Avoid telling a person they are wrong. If you must, do it in a non-critical way without making a person feel

small.

We always want to prove that we are right, and the other person is wrong. Nothing is accomplished by proving a person wrong. It only damages their inner regard for you. It also strips their self-dignity and ego.

The reverse holds true, too. In our own case, if we are in the wrong, we should admit it right away.

17. If you have to give a lecture or a speech, try to inject humour into it. If you need to make a joke, turn it around and make yourself the butt of the joke.

In Air India, it was mandatory for the in-flight supervisor (IFS) to assemble all the crew members in the special briefing room, next to the cabin crew movement control office before a flight out, and brief them about various aspects of the upcoming flight.

The briefing could be on any topic; about emergency procedures and the various emergency equipment and their locations on board, a rapid review of various topics pertaining to the flight. Most crew members came to the briefing room thinking, "Okay, one more boring lecture before the flight."

When I became an in-flight supervisor (IFS), I reminded the crew that if we were a team of sixteen cabin crew members on board a 747 flight, we probably had about 160+ years of flying experience between all of us (assuming an average length of service of about ten years per every crew member). With that much experience was a 'pre-flight briefing' really necessary?

My briefing was, "Just be happy. Keep the passengers happy. Do your work. Do the liquor and meal service. Take a break. Relax a bit and get back for the second service (if any). Most importantly enjoy your work and your flight. If we are all happy and smiling, the passengers will be happy and smiling, too! If any passenger has a problem, or is unhappy and upset, call me."

I always ended the briefing with a new joke or two, or some funny incidents from previous flights. The crew loved it.

If the time of arrival at the destination was not at some unearthly hour, I announced a non-mandatory get together in the hotel crew room after the flight.

18. Make the other person feel relevant, crucial, and important, and mean it.

If you can follow these few tips and suggestions and incorporate them into your new lifestyle, you, too, will see a SAARO MANAS in everyone.

With the change in your approach to people, they too will change the way they react to you, and you will witness a different world. Do this over a period of time, and it will become a habit and a part of your lifestyle. Good habits stay with you forever.

My Master Key has worked for me most of my life, and I see no reason why it should not work for others. Live a good, happy, fulfilled, positive, and prosperous life!

37

Hissing Cobra or Deflated Balloon?

Just when I was putting this book to bed, another incident reared up which almost blew this book and me up in flames.

We had a late dinner because I was reviewing the previous chapter, and what I thought would be the last chapter. After dinner, I was watching television with Maloo while the household staff were winding up for the day. One of their last tasks is to warm up drinking water for Maloo for the night and pour it into a flask. But when the maid switched on the stove, the gas cylinder was empty. No big deal. Every household has two cylinders. So she brought in the standby cylinder and moved the regulator from the empty one to the full one. Immediately a hissing sound emitted from the cylinder. It sounded like a huge balloon deflating or with a wild stretch of imagination, the hissing of a cobra.

Under normal circumstances, I am usually deaf to low decibel sounds, and my nose rarely detects odors that are subtle and mild. But when I am writing, all my five senses are on duty – following the tenet of *write with all five senses*. So when I was summoned to the kitchen, my nose and ears were young again. The odor in the kitchen told me there was no cobra hissing behind the cylinder. Neither were balloons deflating. There was a gas leak from the new gas cylinder.

First, I detached the connector and the pipe. The hissing sound continued. The maids opened all the windows and the main doors, front and rear. My maid suggested that we dribble a few drops of water on the cylinder valve to check if any bubbles poured out, confirming the leak. We tried it and confirm it did!

Immediately, I called 1906 - the emergency number to call for help in a gas leakage situation. Surprise, surprise! A sweet pre-recorded female voice wanted to know my language preference. Hindi, Marathi or English? At that point my language preference was &*!#*!. The slow and monotonous voice continued, informing me of all the different functions available, in case I was a new and perspective honored customer. I wanted to scream abuse into the mobile, my Parsi profanities and the English four-letter words. And I did!!!

I switched 'off' the chatty lady at the other end and called my other emergency number - my daughter Jennifer and my son-in-law Serge. A live voice with immediate instructions:

Detach the gas regulator! Check.

Open all windows! Check.

Everyone get out of the kitchen! Check.

Don't touch any electric switches! Check.

Next minute, my dearest Shovir, my go-to man, called. He told me he was on his way and would send a gas cylinder mechanic over in minutes and for everyone to stay away, far, far away from the kitchen.

Jennifer, with her husband, Serge covered the distance from Colaba to Napean Sea Road in nine minutes like a Grand Prix race driver. A drive that would normally take thirty minutes. The first thing Serge did was take the cylinder out of the house. He carried the cylinder two floors up to the terrace.

Minutes later, Shovir, my always-there-for-you man, was there at the door, driving at break-neck speed, faster than any fire brigade, all the way from Bandra. He brought with him a uniformed gas cylinder mechanic, tool kit in hand. Shovir and the mechanic joined Jennifer and Serge on the terrace. The bomb squad had arrived. The bomb was defused.

What if the cylinder had actually burst?

My daughter Jennifer, and my two sons, Serge and Shovir, endangered their own lives to save their parents' lives. That, in my book, is love.

The next morning, I wondered if I had imagined the endless loop in the 1906 interactive voice response system. I dialed the emergency number 1906 one more time, just to test the response. And sure enough the sweet, recorded voice at the other end, wanted to know in which language, Hindi, Marathi or English, would I like to converse in. Unfortunately, I did not know the Hindi nor the Marathi word to cry out and holler S.O.S. At my age, I don't have the time to dance my way down the endless loop of automated voice systems. I can only express my frustration as another chapter in my book.

Epilogue

Air India: The Palace in the Sky

It was 15th October 1932. Twenty-eight-year-old, Jehangir Ratanji Dadabhoy (JRD) Tata, clad in his hallmark outfit – white trousers and short-sleeved shirt - paced the hallways of aviation waiting for the birth of his soon-to-be cherished child. When the 25 kg child was born, JRD hauled it into a single engine de Havilland Puss Moth and flew it from Karachi to Bombay. Thus, was born Tata Airlines. The much-awaited delivery resulted in a 25-kg bag of mail.

For fourteen years JRD (or Jeh, as he was called) nursed, nourished, reared, and brought up the love of his life, Tata Airlines, in his image – adventurous, suave, humble and down to earth. When he, reluctantly, let it fly the coop in 1946, his child burst forth into the world as a Maharaja - the Air India Maharaja.

The credit for creating the Maharaja, giving him a personality, building him up as a brand, goes to Bobby Kooka, the Commercial

Director of Air India, and artist Umesh Rao.

The Maharaja was Air India's lucky mascot: with the twirled up extra-long moustache on a chubby round face with a Parsi nose, a striped red-and-white Indian turban, with folded hands, and/or with one hand on his heart in a bow giving you a warm welcome with 'doors always wide open.'

In 1948, with the launch of 'Air India International', the Air India logo was born: the Zodiac sign of Sagittarius the Archer, in a circle. The image denoted speed and the right direction. The whole world knew that the Sagittarian Centaur belonged to Air India.

Tata Airlines was created about a decade before I was born. By the time I grew up and started my career there, it had become Air India.

In the 1960s, Air India became the first Asian airline to introduce an all-Jet fleet, when it took delivery of its first 707 Boeing. The AI 707 fleet was named after the different mountain peaks of the Himalayan range.

About a decade later, Air India introduced its fleet of 747 Jumbo jets. This time the 747 Jumbo fleet was named after the Maharajahs of yester years. The Air India Maharajah became the Emperor and Monarch of the skies with a slogan *Your Palace in the Sky*. Every window of the fuselage and cabin was decorated and embellished to look like a palace. The beautiful interiors were alluring, colorful, and the fascinating visuals were intricately designed reflecting true Indian heritage. The interior and exterior of the aircraft became world famous.

On long haul flights, discerning passengers sipped champagne or whisky in crystal glasses, admiring the wall prints and murals, comprising of rich tapestries, age-old art of ancient Indian motifs. They were served by air hostesses wearing ceremoniously decorated Rajasthani *Ghaghra-Choli* outfits, eye-catching Indian jewelry and ornaments, and they tip-toed in Rajasthani *mojeries* - gold threaded and embroidered footwear. They looked exotic to the first class and executive class elite VIP passengers who thought they were goddesses in the sky.

The first-class cabin had a unique, one-of-a-kind upper lounge with a bar of exotic French wines, Dom Perignon, Veuve Clicquot champagnes, and the best brands of liquor and liqueurs of the world. Blue Label whisky, French Cognac, Bordeaux & Burgundy wines flowed like water, accompanied by cold canapes, Swiss & Danish cheeses, hors d'oeuvres and mouthwatering hot appetizers. It was truly a banquet for royalty.

I had a 38-year career in Air India – the best years of my life. Air India had become a part of my body and soul. Sometimes it felt like Air India permeated out of every limb of mine: an extra appendage to my body. I loved and enjoyed my job so much, that I proved Confucius right: *If you love what you do, you will not work a single day in your life.* Sometimes I felt like I wore Air India like Superman's cloak around me: with anyone I met or anywhere I went, the catch phrase was *He is with Air India, or He flies for Air India.* I felt like the Maharaja was stamped on my heart and the Sagittarian Centaur was stitched on my sleeve.

In 1999, I decided it was time to hang up my boots. Everything in my life had to be momentous and larger than life. The same can be said for the date of my retirement. 31st December 1999. The last month of the year, the last day of the year, the last day of the century, the last day of the millennium. When the entire world was waiting with bated breath to see if all computer programs would work for Y2K – the turnover of the century: if life-saving medical equipment would stop working; if airplanes would fall out of the sky; and so on I picked that day to hang up my Air India uniform cap on a thirty-eight-year career at Air India.

Was I the only one asking "Y 2 Go, Y 2 Go? And where to go??" It was the end of the road for me. At the stroke of midnight on the 31st of December 1999, I ceased to be an Air Indian.

A long innings and the saddest day of my life.

In those thirty-eight years, I had been a junior cargo assistant, senior traffic assistant, assistant flight purser, flight purser, senior check flight purser, an in-flight supervisor, and finally a senior manager, in-flight service department. Thanks to Air India, I had several overseas postings and, my family and I had the good fortune to be exposed to different countries and cultures for long periods of time. At other times, I was at the base station in Bombay and flew out to various international destinations for a week or so. Back in Bombay, I was not on duty until the next flight, and that gave me time with my family.

I left my dream job with a million memories - mostly good and at times, excellent. If I had to live my life all over again, give me the very same job with the very same colleagues and friends, and of course, the very same airline. My airline has given me so much. Far, far more than any expectations I ever had.

Today, there are 9,500 happy and proud employees in Air India, and 50,000 content and grateful retired employees of Air India. That makes almost 60,000 in the Air India family in the world today.

Sixty-nine years later, Air India is back with the Tata group. Back again with the founders of Air India after 69 years! Yes, 69 long years. A full circle. And what a circle it has been! If at all anyone can bring those colorful and golden days back, it would be the Tata group. The legendary airline has landed smoothly on the right runaway. Back home.

Air India going back to the Tata group is the most nonpareil thing that could happen to Air India and to Indian aviation. It is not only the *cherry on the cake,* but the entire cake. It is not only the *cream of the crop,* but the crème de la crème of aviation.

The Tatas are not just a great business house. They are humane, benevolent, generous and charitable to the core. They are compassionate, gracious to their employees and guests, on land, and high up in the skies.

27th January 2022 will go down as the biggest day in the airline industry in India. The biological parents, the Tatas took back their 69-year-old ailing child from the hands of foster parents and their caretakers - the Government of yesteryears. Self-centered, shady, self-profiteering and unethical foster parents and their designated caretakers, who misused their avariciously adopted child. Pillage, plunder, inappropriate and incorrect decisions crippled their child, Air India.

Looking back, if the Government of India had not nationalized Air India all those years ago, if JRD Tata, Ratan Tata and the Tata group would have continued to raise their own baby all these years, where would the airline be? Where would its employees be today? Each and every employee of Air India, past, present and future would have been a Maharaja today; and, their families would have lived king-sized lives. The Airline would have stayed on the top of the aviation world, wearing the golden crown of the Maharaja. The potential boggles the mind.

Air India may be debt ridden today, but the Tata stamp on it is already making waves.

The Chairman of Tata & Sons, Mr. N. Chandrasekaran has promised that the Tata group will not only bring Air India out of the red but will make it financially robust again. The Tatas will upgrade its aircrafts, buy a brand-new fleet, and make Air India devotedly, affectionately, and technologically the most advanced airline. Every passenger will know how very special it felt, to be on board and fly Air India. One more time Air India shall soar high into the skies, reclaim its place as a *Palace in the Sky:* "Flying High"!!

With the Tatas at the helm, *better days are a comin'.*

> *Oh, I know that there'll be better days*

> *Oh, that sunshine 'bout to come my way*

I wish I was a few decades younger to take part in this new avatar of Air India and enjoy another adventurous journey in the skies.

This is my tribute and my sincere gratitude to JRD Tata and the Tata group for giving me and my family so much in our lives. We owe our successes in life to them.

God bless the Tata group. God bless Air India and all its employees of yesteryears, today and tomorrow. God bless the safe travels for its every passenger and crew member, worldwide.

Thank you, dear reader.

I hope my book has given you as much pleasure reading it, as I have had in writing it.

My life has been awash with delightful and varied memoirs, amassed with merriment, fun, frolic and laughter. I have had a few poignant and heart wrenching experiences. Some devastating and catastrophic. Some magical, filled with real-time miracles. Others brimming with love, life-long friendships, absorbing emotions, and a few swift, unforeseen and life-changing twists of fate. In this book, I have tried to narrate as many of my 'once in a life-time' adventures and experiences with historical accuracy. I have also shared my personal philosophy and the tenets by which I have lived and continue to live my life.

Thank you for choosing my book. I sincerely wish it has been worth your while. Whether you liked it or not, I would love to hear from you.

noshirsanjana1@gmail.com

With gratitude

Noshir N. Sanjana

www.ingramcontent.com/pod-product-compliance
Lightning Source LLC
Chambersburg PA
CBHW031126130726
47988CB00006B/2239